CW00369866

Key to Favell's Practical Bookkeeping and Accounts

Second Edition

by M. Chahin, A.C.I.S., M.B.I.M.
Formerly Lecturer in Accountancy, Ealing Technical College

University Tutorial Press Ltd
842 Yeovil Road, Slough, SL1 4JQ

Published by University Tutorial Press Ltd.
842 Yeovil Road, Slough, SL1 4JQ

All rights reserved. No portion of the book
may be reproduced by any process without
written permission from the publishers.

Published 1972
Second Edition 1980
Reprinted 1984, 1985

© M. Chahin 1972, 1980

ISBN 0 7231 0804 8

Printed in Great Britain by
Richard Clay (The Chaucer Press) Ltd
Bungay, Suffolk

Also Available:

Practical Bookkeeping and Accounts

by A. J. Favell, B.Sc. (Econ.), A.C.I.S.
Seventh Edition
Complete course
Part 1 (Elementary course)

Introduction

This Key to Favell's *Practical Bookkeeping and Accounts* is in one respect also a supplement to the textbook. The Vertical form of the Final Accounts and Balance Sheet has been introduced as an alternative to the conventional method at an early stage. I have ventured to do this because most examining bodies welcome this form (although they do not yet insist upon it), and so an increasing number of teachers are introducing it to their students and pupils. The advantage of this form is that it facilitates the understanding or interpretation of Final Accounts and the Balance Sheet.

The alternative treatment of the Journal entries on Purchasing a Business by a Partnership or a Limited Company (Chapters 33 and 41) has the merit of being more concise than that of the textbook method.

Publisher's note to the second edition

This book has been fully revised to reflect changes made in Favell's *Practical Bookkeeping and Accounts* (Seventh Edition). These changes aim at improving the coverage and sequence of the topics, whilst retaining the style and content of earlier editions. The main revisions are:

(a) New chapters have been added on accounting systems, flow charts and internal control (Ch. 16); funds flow statements (Ch. 30); and standard accounting practices (Ch. 43).

(b) The chapter on Control Accounts (Ch. 13) has been brought forward to follow the initial treatment of sales, purchases and related matters.

(c) The chapters on partnership accounting (Chs. 33–36) have been brought together.

(d) The chapters on depreciation (Ch. 22), manufacturing accounts (Ch. 29) and mechanised accounting (Ch. 31) have been completely rewritten.

(e) The sequence of some other chapters has been altered and some sections of the text have been moved to different chapters to improve the flow and development of ideas in the book.

(f) Relevant changes in the law affecting accounts and in good accounting practice have been included up to the date of revision.

(g) Monetary values have been increased in recognition of inflation, although even the revised figures may not long reflect reality.

(h) Some new terminology has been introduced, as well as a modern style for the setting out of the books of account.

The publishers are particularly grateful to Mr. A. Drysdale who reworked many of the solutions set out in the book.

Contents

Chapter 1   Exercises

1   Solution listed on page 1 (*a*) to (*i*) in textbook.

2 and 3   Solution listed on page 2.

Chapter 2   Exercises

1

Cash

19..			£	19..			£
Jan. 1	Capital:			Jan. 10	Purchases		72
	F. Watson		140	17	,,		20
14	Sales		27	21	Expenses:		
16	,,		60		Advertising		15
20	,,		50				

Capital—F. Watson

19..			£	19..			£
				Jan. 1	Cash		140

Purchases

19..			£	19..			£
Jan. 10	Cash		72				
17	,,		20				

Sales

19..			£	19..			£
				Jan. 14	Cash		27
				16	,,		60
				20	,,		50

Expenses

19..			£	19..			£
Jan. 21	Cash:						
	Advertising		15				

2

Cash

19..		£	19..		£
Oct. 1	Capital:		Oct. 1	Purchases	160
	T. Williams	1 000	10	Expenses:	
3	Sales	64		Advertising	10
4	,,	32			
5	,,	64			
7	,,	96			

Capital—T. Williams

19..		£	19..		£
			Oct. 1	Cash	1 000

Purchases

19..		£	19..		£
Oct. 1	Cash	160			

Sales

19..		£	19..		£
			Oct. 3	Cash	64
			4	,,	32
			5	,,	64
			7	,,	96

Expenses

19..		£	19..		£
Oct. 10	Cash:				
	Advertising	10			

3

Cash

19..		£	19..		£
June 1	Capital:		June 1	Purchases	200
	J. Dunbar	900	5	,,	480
8	Sales	1 500	10	Expenses:	
9	,,	1 600		Carriage	40

Capital—J. Dunbar

19..		£	19..		£
			June 1	Cash	900

Purchases

19..			£	19..			£
June 1	Cash		200				
5	,,		480				

Sales

19..			£	19..			£
				June 8	Cash		1 500
				9	,,		1 600

Expenses

19..			£	19..			£
June 10	Cash:						
	Carriage		40				

4

Cash

19..			£	19..			£
Dec. 1	Capital:			Dec. 1	Purchases		550
	J. Bennett		700	12	Expenses:		
6	Sales		200		Carriage		20
8	,,		240	15	Wages		50
14	,,		250				

Capital—J. Bennett

19..			£	19..			£
				Dec. 1	Cash		700

Purchases

19..			£	19..			£
Dec. 1	Cash		550				

Sales

19..			£	19..			£
				Dec. 6	Cash		200
				8	,,		240
				14	,,		250

Expenses

19..			£	19..			£
Dec. 12	Cash:						
	Carriage		20				
15	Wages		50				

5

Cash

19..			£	19..			£
April 1	Capital: H. W. Harrod		560	April 1	Purchases		400
8	Sales		60	3	,,		50
10	,,		80	4	Expenses: Repairs		20
14	,,		220		Carriage		30
19	,,		240				

Capital—H. W. Harrod

19..			£	19..			£
				April 1	Cash		560

Purchases

19..			£	19..			£
April 1	Cash		400				
3	,,		50				

Sales

19..			£	19..			£
				April 8	Cash		60
				10	,,		80
				14	,,		220
				19	,,		240

Expenses

19..			£	19..			£
April 4	Cash: Repairs		20				
	Carriage		30				

6 See pages 8, 9 in textbook.

7 See page 9

8 See page 10

9 See page 9

Chapter 3   Exercises

1

Cash

19..			£	19..				£
Oct. 1	Capital:			Oct. 2	Purchases			78
	G. Pearce		840	6	Expenses:			
4	Sales		56		Advertising			30
10	,,		113	8	Postage			10
				9	Purchases			37
				10	Balance	c/d		854
			£1 009					£1 009
11	Balance	b/d	854					

Capital—G. Pearce

19..			£	19..			£
Oct. 10	Balance	c/d	854	Oct. 1	Cash		840
				10	Net Profit		14
			£854				£854
				11	Balance	b/d	854

Purchases

19..			£	19..		£
Oct. 2	Cash		78	Oct. 10	Transferred to	
9	,,		37		Trading A/c	115
			£115			£115

Sales

19..		£	19..		£
Oct. 10	Transferred to		Oct. 4	Cash	56
	Trading A/c	169	10	,,	113
		£169			£169

Expenses

19..		£	19..		£
Oct. 6	Cash:		Oct. 10	Transferred to	
	Advertising	30		Profit and	
8	Postage	10		Loss A/c	40
		£40			£40

Trading Account

19.. Oct. 10			£	19.. Oct. 10			£
	Purchases		115		Sales		169
	Gross Profit		54				
			£169				£169

Profit and Loss Account

19.. Oct. 10			£	19.. Oct. 10			£
	Expenses		40		Gross Profit		54
	Net Profit						
	trans. to						
	Capital A/c		14				
			£54				£54

Balance Sheet
as at 10th October, 19..

CLAIMS	£	£	ASSETS	£
Capital	840		Cash in hand	854
Add Net Profit	14			
	—	854		

2

Cash

19.. Dec. 15			£	19.. Dec. 15			£
	Capital:				Purchases		1 400
	J. Leatherhead		1 700	17	Expenses:		
18	Sales		1 250		Stationery		110
20	,,		500	20	Fares, etc.		20
				20	Drawings		150
				20	Balance	c/d	1 770
			£3 450				£3 450
21	Balance	b/d	1 770				

Capital—J. Leatherhead

19.. Dec. 20			£	19.. Dec. 15			£
	Drawings		150		Cash		1 700
	Balance	c/d	1 770	20	Net Profit		220
			£1 920				£1 920
				21	Balance	b/d	1 770

Drawings—J. Leatherhead

19..		£	19..		£
Dec. 20	Cash	150	Dec. 20	Transferred to Capital A/c	150

Purchases

19..		£	19..		£
Dec. 15	Cash	1 400	Dec. 20	Transferred to Trading A/c	1 400

Sales

19..		£	19..		£
Dec. 20	Transferred to Trading A/c	1 750	Dec. 18	Cash	1 250
			20	,,	500
		£1 750			£1 750

Expenses

19..		£	19..		£
Dec. 17	Cash: Stationery	110	Dec. 20	Transferred to Profit and Loss A/c	130
20	Fares, etc.	20			
		£130			£130

Trading Account

19..		£	19..		£
Dec. 20	Purchases	1 400	Dec. 20	Sales	1 750
	Gross Profit	350			
		£1 750			£1 750

Profit and Loss Account

19..		£	19..		£
Dec. 20	Expenses	130	Dec. 20	Gross Profit	350
	Net Profit trans. to Capital A/c	220			
		£350			£350

Balance Sheet
as at 20th December, 19 . .

CLAIMS	£	£	ASSETS	£
Capital	1 700		Cash in hand	1 770
Add Net Profit	220			
	1 920			
Less Drawings	150			
		1 770		
		£1 770		£1 770

3   Gross Profit £50; No Profit or Loss; Balance Sheets total £300.

4   Gross Profit £240; Net Profit £195; Balance Sheet totals £900.

5   Gross Profit £59; Net Profit £40; Balance Sheet totals £1 010.

6   See pages 15 and 21 in textbook.

Chapter 4   Exercises

1

Cash

19 . .			£	19 . .			£
Mar. 16	Capital:			Mar. 16	Purchases		1 350
	J. Filmer		2 000	17	,,		130
19	Sales		750	17	Expenses		10
20	,,		1 030	20	,,		10
				20	Balance	c/d	2 280
			£3 780				£3 780
21	Balance	b/d	2 280				

Capital—J. Filmer

19 . .			£	19 . .			£
Mar. 20	Balance	c/d	2 500	Mar. 16	Cash		2 000
				20	Net Profit		500
			£2 500				£2 500
				21	Balance	b/d	2 500

Purchases

19 . .			£	19 . .			£
Mar. 16	Cash		1 350	Mar. 20	Transferred to		
17	,,		130		Trading A/c		1 480
			£1 480				£1 480

Sales

19 . .			£	19 . .			£
Mar. 20	Transferred to			Mar. 19	Cash		750
	Trading A/c		1 780	20	,,		1 030
			£1 780				£1 780

Expenses

19 . .			£	19 . .			£
Mar. 17	Cash		10	Mar. 20	Transferred to		
20	,,		10		Profit and		
					Loss A/c		20
			£20				£20

Stock

19 . .			£	19 . .			£
Mar. 20	Trading A/c		220				

Trading and Profit and Loss Account
for period ended 20th March, 19 . .

19 . .			£	19 . .			£
	Purchases		1 480		Sales		1 780
	Less Closing						
	Stock		220				
	Cost of Sales		1 260				
	Gross Profit	c/d	520				
			£1 780				£1 780
	Expenses		20		Gross Profit	b/d	520
	Net Profit						
	transferred						
	to Capital						
	A/c		500				
			£520				£520

Balance Sheet
as at 20th March, 19..

CLAIMS	£	£	ASSETS	£
Capital	2 000		Stock 20th March	220
Add Net Profit	500		Cash in hand	2 280
		2 500		
		£2 500		£2 500

2   Gross Profit £370; Net Profit £310; Balance Sheet totals £1 810.

3

Cash

19..			£	19..			£
Sept. 2	Capital: J. Sharp		1 000	Sept. 2	Purchases		800
8	Sales		500	2	,,		80
10	,,		400	2	Expenses: Carriage		10
				3	Packing Materials		20
				10	Balance	c/d	990
			£1 900				£1 900
11	Balance	b/d	990	11	Purchases		700
15	Sales		520	12	Expenses: Carriage		20
16	,,		600	16	Drawings		200
				16	Balance	c/d	1 190
			£2 110				£2 110
17	Balance	b/d	1 190				

Capital—J. Sharp

19..			£	19..			£
Sept. 10	Balance	c/d	1 350	Sept. 2	Cash		1 000
					Net Profit		350
			£1 350				£1 350
16	Drawings		200	11	Balance	b/d	1 350
	Balance	c/d	1 450	16	Net Profit		300
			£1 650				£1 650
				17	Balance	b/d	1 450

Drawings—J. Sharp

19..		£	19..		£
Sept. 16	Cash	200	Sept. 16	Transferred to Capital A/c	200

Purchases

19..		£	19..		£
Sept. 2	Cash	800	Sept. 10	Transferred to Trading A/c	880
2	,,	80			
		£880			£880
11	Cash	700	16	Transferred to Trading A/c	700

Sales

19..		£	19..		£
Sept. 10	Transferred to Trading A/c	900	Sept. 8	Cash	500
			10	,,	400
		£900			£900
16	Transferred to Trading A/c	1 120	15	Cash	520
			16	,,	600
		£1 120			£1 120

Expenses

19..		£	19..		£
Sept. 2	Cash: Carriage	10	Sept. 10	Transferred to Profit and Loss A/c	30
	Packing Materials	20			
		£30			£30
12	Cash: Carriage	20	16	Transferred to Profit and Loss A/c	20

Stock

19..		£	19..		£
			Sept. 16	Transferred to Trading A/c	360
Sept. 10	Trading A/c	360			
16	Trading A/c	260			

Trading and Profit and Loss Account
for period ended 10th September, 19..

19..			£	19..			£
	Purchases		880		Sales		900
	Less Closing						
	Stock		360				
	Cost of Sales		520				
	Gross Profit	c/d	380				
			£900				£900
	Expenses		30		Gross Profit	b/d	380
	Net Profit						
	transferred						
	to Capital						
	A/c		350				
			£380				£380

Balance Sheet
as at 10th September, 19..

CLAIMS	£	£	ASSETS	£
Capital	1 000		Stock 10th September	360
Add Net Profit	350		Cash in hand	990
		1 350		
		£1 350		£1 350

Trading and Profit and Loss Account
for period ended 16th September, 19..

19..			£	19..			£
	Opening Stock				Sales		1 120
	11th Sept.		360				
	Purchases		700				
	Less Closing		1 060				
	Stock		260				
	Cost of Sales		800				
	Gross Profit	c/d	320				
			£1 120				£1 120
	Expenses		20		Gross Profit	b/d	320
	Net Profit						
	trans. to						
	Capital A/c		300				
			£320				£320

Balance Sheet
as at 16th September, 19 . .

CLAIMS	£	£	ASSETS	£
Capital	1 350		Stock 16th September	260
Add Net Profit	300		Cash in hand	1 190
	1 650			
Less Drawings	200			
		1 450		
		£1 450		£1 450

4 Oct. 1–18. Cash, Purchases, Sales, Expenses Accounts as in No. 3.

Capital—J. Plater

19 . . Oct. 18	Net Loss Balance	c/d	£ 100 9 900	19 . . Oct. 1	Cash	£ 10 000
			£10 000			£10 000
				19	Balance	9 900

Trading and Profit and Loss Account
for period ended 18th October, 19 . .

19 . .			£	19 . .			£
	Purchases		9 200		Sales		7 600
	Less Closing Stock		1 700				
	Cost of Sales		7 500				
	Gross Profit	c/d	100				
			£7 600				£7 600
	Expenses		200		Gross Profit	b/d	100
					Net Loss trans. to Capital A/c		100
			£200				£200

Balance Sheet
as at 18th October, 19..

CLAIMS	£	£		ASSETS	£
Capital	10 000			Stock 18th October	1 700
Less Net Loss	100			Cash	8 200
		9 900			
		£9 900			£9 900

Oct. 19–31. Gross Profit £3 500; Net Profit £3 400; Balance Sheet totals £11 300.

5 Nov. 1–8. Gross Profit £660; Net Profit £530; Balance Sheet totals £2 380.
Nov. 9–30. Gross Profit £570; Net Profit £390; Balance Sheet totals £2 770.

Chapter 5   Exercises

1

Cash

19..			£	19..			£
Jan. 1	Capital:			Jan. 1	Purchases		6 000
	J. White		10 000	6	Expenses:		
19	F. Lawson		5 000		Carriage		300
				31	Expenses		500
					Balance	c/d	8 200
			£15 000				£15 000
Feb. 1	Balance	b/d	8 200				

Capital—J. White

19..			£	19..			£
Jan. 31	Balance	c/d	13 700	Jan. 1	Cash		10 000
				31	Net Profit		3 700
			£13 700				13 700
				Feb. 1	Balance	b/d	13 700

Purchases

19..			£	19..			£
Jan. 1	Cash		6 000	Jan. 31	Trans. to		
16	Motor Equip-		9 000		Trading A/c		15 000
	ment Co.						
			£15 000				£15 000

Sales

19.. Jan. 31	Trans. to Trading A/c		£ 19 200	19.. Jan. 2 23 27	F. Lawson B. Coombes F. Lawson		£ 5 000 7 000 7 200
			£19 200				£19 200

F. Lawson

19.. Jan. 2 27	Sales ,,		£ 5 000 7 200	19.. Jan. 19 31	Cash Balance	c/d	£ 5 000 7 200
			£12 200				£12 200
Feb. 1	Balance	b/d	7 200				

B. Coombes

19.. Jan. 23	Sales		£ 7000	19..			£

Motor Equipment Co.

19..			£	19.. Jan. 16	Purchases		£ 9000

Expenses

19.. Jan. 6 31	Cash ,,		£ 300 500	Jan. 31	Trans. to Profit and Loss A/c		800
			£800				£800

Stock

19.. Jan. 31	Trading A/c		£ 300	19..			£

Trading and Profit and Loss Account
for month ended 31st January, 19..

19..			£	19..			£
	Purchases		15 000		Sales		19 200
	Less Closing Stock		300				
	Cost of Sales		14 700				
	Gross Profit	c/d	4 500				
			£19 200				£19 200
	Expenses		800		Gross Profit	b/d	4 500
	Net Profit trans. to Capital A/c		3 700				
			£4 500				£4 500

Balance Sheet
as at 31st January, 19..

CLAIMS	£	£	ASSETS	£
Capital	10 000		Stock 31st January	300
Add Net Profit	3 700		Sundry Debtors	14 200
		13 700	Cash in hand	8 200
Sundry Creditors		9 000		
		£22 700		£22 700

2   Gross Profit £390; Net Profit £310; Balance Sheet totals £1 510.

3

Cash

19..			£	19..			£
June 1	Capital: J. Shaw		1 700	June 2	Purchases		1 200
15	Sales		1 190	4	Expenses: Carriage		70
				15	Balance	c/d	1 620
			£2 890				£2 890
16	Balance	b/d	1 620	21	Camp Supplies Ltd.		1 500
28	Smith Stores		2 400	30	Expenses		40
				30	Drawings		400
				30	Balance	c/d	2 080
			£4 020				£4 020
July 1	Balance	b/d	2 080				

Capital—J. Shaw

19.. June 15	Balance	c/d	£ 2 360	19.. June 1 16	Cash Net Profit	T	£ 1 700 660
			£2 360				£2 360
30	Drawings Balance	T c/d	400 2 280	16 30	Balance Net Profit	b/d T	2 360 320
			£2 680				£2 680
				July 1	Balance	b/d	2 280

Drawings—J. Shaw

19.. June 30	Cash		£ 400	19.. June 30	Capital	T	£ 400

Purchases

19.. June 1 2	Camp supplies Ltd. Cash		£ 1 500 1 200	19.. June 15	Trading A/c	T	£ 2 700
			£2 700				£2 700
22	Camp supplies Ltd.		1 200	30	Trading A/c	T	1 200

'T' = Balance transferred (e.g. to Trading A/c)

Sales

19.. June 15	Trading A/c	T	£ 2 590	19.. June 10 15	Smith's Stores Ltd. Cash		£ 1 400 1 190
			£2 590				£2 590
30	Trading A/c	T	1 000	16	Smith's Stores Ltd.		1 000

Expenses

19.. June 4	Cash		£ 70	19.. June 15	Profit and Loss A/c	T	£ 70
30	Cash		40	30	Profit and Loss A/c	T	40

Stock

19..			£	19..			£
June 15	Trading A/c		840	June 30	Trading A/c	T	840
30	Trading A/c		1 400				

Camp Supplies Ltd.

19..			£	19..			£
June 21	Cash		1 500	June 1	Purchases		1 500
30	Balance	c/d	1 200	22	,,		1 200
			£2 700				£2 700
				July 1	Balance	b/d	1 200

Smith's Stores Ltd.

19..			£	19..		£
June 10	Sales		1 400	June 28	Cash	2 400
16	,,		1 000			
			£2 400			£2 400

Trading and Profit and Loss Account
for 2 weeks ended 15th June, 19..

19..			£	19..			£
	Purchases		2 700		Sales		2 590
	Less Closing Stock		840				
	Cost of Sales		1 860				
	Gross Profit	c/d	730				
			£2 590				£2 590
	Expenses:				Gross Profit	b/d	730
	Carriage		70				
	Net Profit trans. to						
	Capital		660				
			£730				£730

Balance Sheet
as at 15th June, 19..

CLAIMS	£	£	ASSETS	£
Capital	1 700		Stock 15th June	840
Add Net Profit	660		Sundry Debtors	1 400
		2 360	Cash	1 620
Sundry Creditors		1 500		
		£3 860		£3 860

Trading and Profit and Loss Account
for 2 weeks ended 30th June, 19 . .

19 . .			£	19 . .			£
	Opening Stock 16th June		840		Sales		1 000
	Purchases		1 200				
			2 040				
	Less Closing Stock		1 400				
	Cost of Sales		640				
	Gross Profit	c/d	360				
			£1 000				£1 000
	Expenses		40		Gross Profit	b/d	360
	Net Profit trans. to Capital		320				
			£360				£360

Balance Sheet
as at 30th June, 19 . .

CLAIMS	£	£	ASSETS	£
Capital	2 360		Stock 30th June	1 400
Add Net Profit	320		Cash	2 080
	2 680			
Less Drawings	400			
		2 280		
Sundry Creditors		1 200		
		£3 480		£3 480

4

Sept. 4–14. Cash £1 890; Gross Profit £480; Net Profit £330; Balance Sheet totals £5 970.

Sept. 15–30. Cash £2 590; Gross Profit £1 300; Net Profit £970; Balance Sheet totals £6 190.

Chapter 6   Exercises

1

Cash

19..			£	19..			£
Dec. 1	Capital:			Dec. 1	Purchases		360
	J. Bentham		900	7	,,		450
17	J. Smith		780	8	Expenses:		
					Packing		
					Materials		10
				31	Expenses		50
				31	Balance	c/d	810
			£1 680				£1 680
Jan. 1	Balance	b/d	810				

Capital—J. Bentham

19..			£	19..			£
Dec. 31	Balance	c/d	1 290	Dec. 1	Cash		900
				31	Net Profit		390
			£1 290				£1 290
				Jan. 1	Balance	b/d	1 290

Purchases

19..			£	19..			£
Dec. 1	Cash		360	Dec. 31	Trading A/c	T	990
3	J. Tobin & Co.		180				
7	Cash		450				
			£990				£990

Sales

19..			£	19..			£
Dec. 31	Trading A/c	T	1 140	Dec. 10	J. Smith		780
				12	W. Wilkins		360
			£1 140				£1 140

Expenses

19..			£	19..			£
Dec. 8	Cash: Packing			Dec. 31	Profit and		
	Materials		10		Loss A/c	T	60
	Cash		50				
			£60				£60

Stock

19..			£	19..			£
Dec. 31	Trading A/c		300				

J. Tobin & Co.

19..			£	19..			£
				Dec. 3	Purchases		180

J. Smith

19..			£	19..			£
Dec. 10	Sales		780	Dec. 17	Cash		780

W. Wilkins

19..			£	19..			£
Dec. 12	Sales		360				

Trial Balance
31st December, 19..

	Dr.	Cr.
	£	£
Cash	810	
Capital		900
Purchases	990	
Sales		1 140
Expenses	60	
J. Tobin		180
W. Wilkins	360	
	£2 220	£2 220

Trading and Profit and Loss Account
for month ended 31st December, 19..

19..			£	19..			£
	Purchases		990		Sales		1 140
	Less Closing Stock		300				
	Cost of Sales		690				
	Gross Profit	c/d	450				
			£1 140				£1 140
	Expenses		60		Gross Profit	b/d	450
	Net Profit to Capital	T	390				
			£450				£450

Balance Sheet
as at 31st December, 19. .

CLAIMS	£	£	ASSETS	£
Capital	900		Stock 31st December	300
Add Net Profit	390		Debtors	360
		1 290	Cash in hand	810
Creditors		180		
		£1 470		£1 470

2   Ledger accounts, proceed as hitherto.

Trial Balance

19th July, 19. .	*Dr.*	*Cr.*
	£	£
Capital		162
Purchases	277	
Sales		196
Expenses	2	
Silk Weavers Ltd.		90
J. Wesley & Sons	30	
H. Boyce	67	
Cash in hand	72	
	£448	£448

Closing Stock £126.
Gross Profit £45; Net Profit £43; Balance Sheet totals £295.

3   Trial Balance totals £31 455; Gross Profit £13 855; Net Profit £13 815; Balance Sheet totals £24 915.

4

Trading and Profit and Loss Account
for month ended 31st December, 19. .

19. .			£	19. .			£
	Purchases		840		Sales		1 000
	Less Closing Stock		240				
	Cost of Sales		600				
	Gross Profit	c/d	400				
			£1 000				£1 000
	Expenses		50		Gross Profit	b/d	400
	Net Profit to Capital		350				
			£400				£400

Balance Sheet
as at 31st December, 19 . .

CLAIMS	£	£	ASSETS	£
Capital	1 100		Stock	240
Add Net Profit	350	1 450	Debtors	1 150
			Cash	210
Creditors		150		
		£1 600		£1 600

5 Gross Profit £320; Net Profit £240; Balance Sheet totals £1 230.

6 See pages 46 and 47 of textbook.

7

Trial Balance
31st December, 19 . .   *Dr.*   *Cr.*

	£	£
Purchases	8 280	
Cash at Bank	1 278	
Drawings	612	
Loan from J. Haylock		500
Loan to J. Smith	100	
Stock in hand 1st January, 19 . .	335	
Returns Inwards	63	
Sales		13 122
Furniture	80	
Freehold Property	2 000	
Sundry Debtors	1 316	
General Expenses	495	
Discount Received		41
Sundry Creditors		1 042
Carriage Outwards	68	
Plant and Machinery	1 412	
Capital		1 334
	£16 039	£16 039

8 See pages 45 and 46 of textbook.

9 See pages 46 and 47 of textbook.

10

Suspense Account

19 . .		£	19 . .		£
	Purchases	20		Trial Balance	
	B. Simpkins	9		error	40
	Sales	11			
		£40			£40

11

Suspense Account

19..		£	19..		£
	Trial Balance			T. Black	27
	error	19		Sales	10
	Sales	18			
		£37			£37

Chapter 7   Exercises

1

Dr.   **Cash Book**

19..			Cash £	Bank £	19..			Cash £	Bank £
April 1	Capital:				April 1	Bank	C	2 200	
	M. Rafter		2 500		13	,,	C	500	
1	Cash	C*		2 200	15	Expenses			
12	Sales		520		24	Stationery		30	
13	Cash	C		500	27	B. Croydon			1 6
28	L. Sussex			100	30	Expenses			
					30	Carriage		100	
					30	Balances	c/d	190	1 0
			£3 020	£2 800				£3 020	£2 8
May 1	Balances	b/d	190	1 050					

*C = Contra

Capital—M. Rafter

19..			£	19..			£
April 30	Balance	c/d	3 140	April 1	Cash		2 500
				30	Net Profit		640
			£3 140				£3 140
				May 1	Balance	b/d	3 140

Purchases

19..			£	19..			£
April 3	B. Croydon		1 600	April 30	Trading A/c	T	2 900
8	T. Brighton		1 300				
			£2 900				£2 900

Sales

19..			£	19..		£
April 30	Trading A/c	T	2 620	April 12	Cash	520
				21	L. Sussex	100
				22	J. Worthing	2 000
			£2 620			£2 620

Expenses

19..			£	19..			£
April 15	Cash		70	April 30	Profit and		
24	Stationery		30		Loss A/c	T	280
30	Expenses		80				
30	Carriage		100				
			£280				£280

Stock

19..			£	19..		£
April 30	Trading A/c		1 200			

B. Croydon

19..			£	19..		£
April 27	Cash		1 600	April 3	Purchases	1 600

T. Brighton

19..			£	19..		£
				April 8	Purchases	1 300

L. Sussex

19..			£	19..			£
April 21	Sales		100	April 28	Cash		100

J. Worthing

April 22	Sales		2 000				

Trial Balance
30th April, 19..   *Dr.*   *Cr.*

	Dr. £	Cr. £
Cash in hand	190	
Cash at Bank	1 050	
Capital		2 500
Purchases and Sales	2 900	2 620
Expenses	280	
T. Brighton		1 300
J. Worthing	2 000	
	£6 420	£6 420

Trading and Profit and Loss Account
for month ended 30th April, 19..

19..			£	19..			£
	Purchases		2 900		Sales		2 620
	Less Closing Stock		1 200				
	Cost of Sales		1 700				
	Gross Profit	c/d	920				
			£2 620				£2 620
	Expenses		280		Gross Profit	b/d	920
	Net Profit to Capital		640				
			£920				£920

Balance Sheet
as at 30th April, 19..

CLAIMS	£	£	ASSETS	£
Capital	2 500		Stock 30th April	1 200
Add Net Profit	640		Debtors	2 000
		3 140	Cash at Bank	1 050
Creditors		1 300	Cash in hand	190
		£4 440		£4 440

2

Trial Balance

31st October, 19..				*Dr.*	*Cr.*
				£	£
Capital					4 200
Drawings				300	
Purchases and Sales				5 180	2 420
Expenses				240	
R. Southwark					2 000
Cash at Bank				2 700	
Cash in hand				200	
				£8 620	£8 620

Capital—J. Pearce

19..			£	19..			£
Oct. 31	Drawings	T	300	Oct. 1	Cash		4 200
	Balance	c/d	4 000	31	Net Profit		100
			£4 300				£4 300
				Nov. 1	Balance	b/d	4 000

Drawings—J. Pearce

19..			£	19..			£
Oct. 30	Cash		300	Oct. 31	Capital	T	300

Gross Profit £340; Net Profit £100; Balance Sheet totals £6 000.

3 Dec. 2–14. Cash Balance £7; Bank Balance £95; Trial Balance £910; Gross Profit £130; Net Profit £112; Balance Sheet totals £612.

Dec. 15–31.

Trial Balance

31st December, 19..				*Dr.*	*Cr.*
				£	£
Capital					612
Purchases and Sales				300	389
Expenses				16	
H. Benson				140	
J. Wilson				336	
Farmer & Co.					300
Stock 15th Dec.				170	
Cash in hand				52	
Cash at Bank				287	
				£1 301	£1 301

Trading and Profit and Loss Account
for 2 weeks ended 31st December, 19..

19..			£	19..			£
	Opening Stock		170		Sales		389
	Purchases		300				
			470				
	Less Closing Stock		90				
	Cost of Sales		380				
	Gross Profit	c/d	9				
			£389				£389
	Expenses		16		Gross Profit	b/d	9
					Net Loss to Capital		7
			£16				£16

Balance Sheet
as at 31st December, 19..

Claims	£	£	Assets	£
Capital	612		Stock 31st December	90
Less Net Loss	7		Debtors	476
		605	Cash at Bank	287
Creditors		300	Cash in hand	52
		£905		£905

4   Cash Balance £50; Bank Balance £3 552; Trial Balance totals £11 157. Gross Profit £957; Net Profit £402; Balance Sheet totals £8 102.

Chapter 8   Exercises

1

Dr.   **Cash Book**   C

19..			Cash £	Bank £	19..			Cash £	Bank £
Jan. 1	Capital:				Jan. 1	Cash	C		200
	J. Whitehouse			2 000	3	Purchases			1 300
1	Bank	C	200		7	Wages		60	
12	Sales			380	14	,,		60	
20	,,		400		16	Postage and			
						Carriage		15	
					21	Wages		60	
					22	Packing			
						Materials		25	
					24	R. Nunn		200	400
					28	Wages		60	
					31	Rent			125
					31	Lighting and			
						Heating		50	
					31	Balances	c/d	70	355
			£600	£2 380				£600	£2 380
Feb. 1	Balances	b/d	70	355					

Capital—J. Whitehouse

19..			£	19..			£
Jan. 1	Balance	c/d	2 075	Jan. 1	Cash		2 000
				31	Net Profit		75
			£2 075				£2 075
				Feb. 1	Balance	b/d	2 075

Purchases

19..			£	19..			£
Jan. 2	R. Nunn		600	Jan. 31	Trading A/c	T	1 900
3	Cash		1 300				
			£1 900				£1 900

Sales

19..			£	19..			£
Jan. 31	Trading A/c	T	1 530	Jan. 12	J. Dunn		750
				12	Cash		380
				20	,,		400
			£1 530				£1 530

Wages

19..			£	19..			£
Jan. 7	Cash		60	Jan. 31	Profit and		
14	,,		60		Loss A/c	T	240
21	,,		60				
28	,,		60				
			£240				£240

Postage and Carriage

19..			£	19..			£
Jan. 16	Cash		15	Jan. 31	Profit and		
					Loss A/c	T	15

Packing Materials

19..			£	19..			£
Jan. 22	Cash		25	Jan. 31	Profit and		
					Loss A/c	T	25

Rent

19..			£	19..			£
Jan. 31	Cash		125	Jan. 31	Profit and		
					Loss A/c	T	125

Lighting and Heating

19..			£	19..			£
Jan. 31	Cash		50	Jan. 31	Profit and		
					Loss A/c	T	50

Stock

19..			£	19..			£
Jan. 31	Trading A/c		900	19..			

R. Nunn

19..			£	19..			£
Jan. 24	Cash		600	Jan. 2	Purchases		600

J. Dunn

19..			£	19..			£
Jan. 12	Sales		750	19..			

Trial Balance

31st January, 19..

	Dr.	Cr.
	£	£
Capital		2 000
Purchases and Sales	1 900	1 530
Wages	240	
Postage and Carriage	15	
Packing Materials	25	
Rent	125	
Lighting and Heating	50	
J. Dunn	750	
Cash in hand	70	
Cash at Bank	355	
	£3 530	£3 530

Trading and Profit and Loss Account

for month ended 31st January, 19..

19..			£	19..			£
	Purchases		1 900		Sales		1 530
	Less Closing Stock		900				
	Cost of Sales		1 000				
	Gross Profit	c/d	530				
			£1 530				£1 530
	Wages		240		Gross Profit	b/d	530
	Packing Materials		25				
	Postage and Carriage		15				
	Rent		125				
	Lighting and Heating		50				
	Net Profit to Capital		75				
			£530				£530

Balance Sheet

as at 31st January, 19..

CLAIMS	£	£	ASSETS	£
Capital	2 000		Stock 31st January	900
Add Net Profit	75		Debtors	750
		2 075	Cash at Bank	70
			Cash in hand	355
		£2 075		£2 075

2 Cash Balance £260; Bank Balance £1 900; Trial Balance totals £4 280; Gross Profit £600; Net Profit £520; Balance Sheet totals £2 600.

3   Cash Balance £33; Bank Balance £347; Trial Balance totals £720; Gross Profit £30; Net Loss £5; Balance Sheet totals £520.

4

Trading and Profit and Loss Account
for year ended 1st December, 19. .

19. .		£		19. .			£
	Opening Stock	2 000					
	Purchases	12 000			Sales		17 200
		14 000					
	Less Closing Stock	1 800					
	Cost of Sales	12 200					
	Gross Profit	c/d	5 000				
		£17 200					£17 200
	Wages	1 000			Gross Profit	b/d	5 000
	Lighting	100					210
	Telephone	210					
	Net Profit to Capital	390					
		£5 000					£5 000

Balance Sheet
as at 31st December, 19. .

CLAIMS	£	£	ASSETS	£
Capital	2 500		Stock, 31st December	1 800
Add Net Profit	3 690		Debtors	2 410
		6 190	Cash at Bank	2 120
Creditors		260	Cash in hand	120
		£6 450		£6 450

5   Trial Balance totals £3 868; Gross Profit £790; Net Profit £491; Balance Sheet totals £1 359.

6   Gross Profit £4 099; Net Profit £1 149; Balance Sheet totals £6 945.

Chapter 9   Exercises

1 and **2**   See pages 68 and 69 of textbook.

3   The Purchases Day Book has been included in this solution for the sake of completion (although the exercise does not require it).

Purchases Day Book					**Sales Day Book**			
19..			£	19..			£	
Jan. 1	Cutlery Manu- facturers Ltd.	9	2 000	Jan.14	J. Beaumont W. Bishop & Sons	6	860	
						7	930	
				27	A. M. Godfrey	8	300	
		10	£2 000			11	£2 090	

	Dr.		**Cash Book**				Cr.	

19..			Cash £	Bank £	19..				Cash £	Bank £
Jan. 1	Capital: J. Purvis	1	400	2 560	Jan. 7	Purchases	10			1 200
22	J. Beaumont	6		860	10	Advertising	3		100	
31	Cash Sales	11	240		31	Rent	4			160
					31	Carriage and Packing	5		30	
					31	Balance	c/d		510	2 060
			£640	£3 420					£640	£3 420
Feb. 1	Balances	b/d	510	2 060						

LEDGER
Capital—J. Purvis[1]

19..			£	19..			£
Jan. 31	Balance	c/d	3 300	Jan. 1	Bank	CB	2 560
				1	Cash	CB	400
				31	Net Profit	T	340
			£3 300				£3 300
				Feb. 1	Balance	b/d	3 300

Stock[2]

19..			£	19..			£
Jan. 31	Trading A/c	T	1 500	19..			

Advertising[3]

19 . .			£	19 . .			£
Jan. 10	Cash	CB	100	Jan. 31	Profit and Loss A/c	T	100

Rent[4]

19 . .			£	19 . .			£
Jan. 31	Cash	CB	160	Jan. 31	Profit and Loss A/c	T	160

Carriage and Packing Materials[5]

19 . .			£	19 . .			£
Jan. 31	Cash	CB	30	Jan. 31	Profit and Loss A/c	T	30

J. Beaumont[6]

19 . .			£	19 . .			£
Jan. 14	Sales	SB	860	Jan. 22	Cash	CB	860

W. Bishop & Sons[7]

19 . .			£	19 . .			£
Jan. 21	Sales	SB	930				

A. M. Godfrey[8]

19 . .			£	19 . .			£
Jan. 27	Sales	SB	300				

Cutlery Manufacturers Ltd.[9]

19 . .			£	19 . .			£
				Jan. 1	Purchases	PB	2 000

Purchases[10]

1 . .			£	19 . .			£
Jan. 7	Cash	CB	1 200	Jan. 31	Trading A/c	T	3 200
31	Goods	PB	2 000				
			£3 200				£3 200

Sales[11]

19..			£	19..			£
Jan. 31	Trading A/c	T	2 330	Jan. 31	Cash	CB	240
				31	Goods	SB	2 090
			£2 330				£2 330

Trial Balance
31st December, 19..

	Dr.	Cr.
	£	£
Capital		2 960
Purchases and Sales	3 200	2 330
Cutlery Manufacturers Ltd.		2 000
W. Bishop & Sons	930	
A. M. Godfrey	300	
Advertising	100	
Rent	160	
Carriage and Packing Materials	30	
Cash in hand	510	
Cash at Bank	2 060	
	£7 290	£7 290

Trading and Profit and Loss Account
for month ended 31st January, 19..

19..			£	19..			£
	Purchases		3 200		Sales		2 330
	Less Closing Stock		1 500				
	Cost of Sales		1 700				
	Gross Profit	c/d	630				
			£2 330				£2 330
	Rent		160		Gross Profit	b/d	630
	Advertising		100				
	Carriage and Packing Materials		30				
	Net Profit to Capital		340				
			£630				£630

Balance Sheet
as at 31st January, 19..

CLAIMS	£	£	ASSETS	£
Capital	2 960		Stock	1 500
Add Net Profit	340		Debtors	1 230
		3 300	Cash at Bank	2 060
Creditors		2 000	Cash in hand	510
		£5 300		£5 300

4 Cash Balance £180; Bank Balance £460; Trial Balance totals £2 990; Gross Profit £170; Net Profit £90; Balance Sheet totals £2 010.

5 Cash Balance £130; Bank Balance £260; Trial Balance totals £3 580; Gross Profit £120; Net Profit £80; Balance Sheet totals £1 530.

6

To illustrate treatment of Returns Inwards

LEDGER (Extract)
B. Johnson

19..			£	19..			£
Nov. 20	Sales	SB	600	Nov. 23	Returns	RIB	100
				30	Cash	CB	500
			£600				£600

B. Beamish & Sons

19..			£	19..			£
Nov. 25	Sales	SB	420	Nov. 27	Returns	RIB	100
				30	Balance	c/d	320
			£420				£420
Nov. 30	Balance	b/d	320				

Returns Inwards

19..			£	19..			£
Nov. 30	Goods	RIB	200	Nov. 30	Sales	T	200

Sales

19..			£	19..			£
Nov. 30	Returns	T	200	Nov. 10	Cash	CB	1 750
30	Trading A/c	T	2 570	30	Goods	SB	1 020
			£2 770				£2 770

Trial Balance

30th November, 19..	*Dr.*	*Cr.*
	£	£
Capital		4 000
Purchases and Sales	4 200	2 770
Returns Inwards	200	
Rent	160	
Printing and Stationery	150	
B. Beamish & Sons	320	
Electrical Supplies Ltd.		1 000
Cash in hand	50	
Cash at Bank	2 690	
	£7 770	£7 770

Trading and Profit and Loss Account
for month ended 30th November, 19..

19..			£	19..			£
	Purchases		4 200		Sales	2 770	
	Less Closing				*Less*		
	Stock		2 370		Returns	200	
							2 570
			1 830				
	Gross Profit	c/d	740				
			£2 570				£2 570
	Rent		160		Gross Profit	b/d	740
	Printing and						
	Stationery		150				
	Net Profit		430				
			£740				£740

Balance Sheet totals: £5 430

7 Cash Balance £1 040; Bank Balance £2 710; Trial Balance totals £8 150; Gross Profit £1 350; Net Profit £1 000; Balance Sheet totals £4 650

8

	Purchases Day Book				**Sales Day Book**		
19..			£	19..			£
Dec. 2	J. Townsend			Dec.10	J. Burton	10	219
	& Sons	9	441			4	£219
21	J. Townsend						
	& Sons	9	162				
		2	£603				

Returns Outwards Book

19..				£
Dec. 23	J. Townsend & Sons	9		15
		3		£15

Returns Inwards Book

19..			£
Dec. 12	J. Burton	10	9
		5	£9

Dr.   **Cash Book**   *Cr.*

19..			Cash £	Bank £	19..			Cash £	Bank £
Dec. 1	Capital: J. M. Biggs	1		750	Dec. 2	Purchases	2		560
7	Sales	4	90		2	Carriage	6		36
12	,,	4		264	19	J. Townsend and Sons	9		441
17	J. Burton	10		210	31	Expenses	7	26	
28	Sales	4		231	31	Balances	c/d	64	418
			£90	£1 455				£90	£1 455
Jan. 1	Balances	b/d	64	418					

Capital—J. M. Biggs[1]

19..			£	19..			£
Dec. 31	Balance	c/d	845	Dec. 1	Cash	CB	750
				31	Net Profit	T	95
			£845				£845
				Jan. 1	Balance	b/d	845

Purchases[2]

19..			£	19..			£
Dec. 2	Cash	CB	560	Dec. 31	Returns	T	15
31	Goods	PDB	603	31	Trading A/c	T	1 148
			£1 163				£1 163

Returns Outwards[3]

19..			£	19..			£
Dec. 31	Purchases	T	15	Dec. 31	Goods	ROB	15

Sales[4]

19..			£	19..			£
Dec. 31	Returns	T	9	Dec. 7	Cash	CB	90
	Trading A/c	T	795	12	,,	CB	264
				28	,,	CB	231
				31	Goods	SDB	219
			£804				£804

Returns Inwards[5]

19..			£	19..		£	
Dec. 31	Goods	RIB	9	Dec. 31	Sales	T	9

Carriage[6]

19..			£	19..			£
Dec. 2	Cash	CB	36	Dec. 31	Profit and Loss A/c	T	36

Expenses[7]

19..			£	19..			£
Dec. 31	Cash	CB	26	Dec. 31	Profit and Loss A/c	T	26

Stock[8]

19..				19..			£
Dec. 31	Trading A/c	T	510				

J. Townsend & Sons[9]

19..			£	19..			£
Dec. 19	Cash	CB	441	Dec. 2	Purchases	PDB	441
23	Returns	ROB	15	21	,,	PDB	162
31	Balance	c/d	147				
			£603				£603
				Jan. 1	Balance	b/d	147

J. Burton[10]

19..			£	19..			£
Dec. 10	Sales	SDB	219	Dec. 12	Returns	RIB	9
				17	Cash	CB	210
			£219				£219

Trial Balance

31st December, 19..	Dr.	Cr.
	£	£
Capital		750
Cash in hand	64	
Cash at Bank	418	
Purchases and Sales	1 163	804
Returns Inwards and Outwards	9	15
Carriage	36	
Expenses	26	
J. Townsend and Sons		147
	£1 716	£1 716

Trading and Profit and Loss Account

for month ended, 31st December, 19..

		£	£			£	£
Purchases		1 163		Sales		804	
Less Returns		15		*Less* Returns		9	
			1 148				795
Less Closing Stock			510				
Cost of Sales			638				
Gross Profit	c/d		157				
			£795				£795
Carriage			36	Gross Profit	b/d		157
Expenses			26				
Net Profit to Capital	T		95				
			£157				£157

Balance Sheet

as at 31st December, 19..

CLAIMS	£	£	ASSETS	£
Capital	750		Stock, 31st December	510
Add Net Profit	95		Cash at Bank	418
		845	Cash in hand	64
Creditors		147		
		£992		£992

9 Cash Balance £170; Bank Balance £5 250; Trial Balance totals £11 780; Gross Profit £1 430; Net Profit £1 090; Balance Sheet totals £7 800.

10 (First Period)

Trial Balance
31st May, 19..

	Dr.	Cr.
	£	£
Capital		300
Cash at Bank	48	
Cash in hand	79	
Purchases	252	
Sales		110
Returns Outwards		24
Electric Supplies Ltd.		32
Baring & Lee	70	
Sundry Expenses	1	
Carriage	16	
	£466	£466

Trading and Profit and Loss Account
for month ended 31st May, 19..

		£	£			£
Purchases		252		Sales		110
Less Returns		24				
			228			
Less Closing Stock			145			
			83			
Gross Profit	c/d		27			
			£110			£110
Sundry Expenses			1	Gross Profit	b/d	27
Carriage			16			
Net Profit to Capital			10			
			£27			£27

Balance Sheet
as at 31st May, 19..

CLAIMS	£	£	ASSETS	s
Capital	300		Stock	145
Add Net Profit	10		Debtors	70
		310	Cash at Bank	48
Creditors		32	Cash in hand	79
		£342		£342

10 (Second Period)

Trial Balance

30th June, 19..	Dr.	Cr.
	£	£
Capital		310
Drawings	40	
Stock 1st June	145	
Sales		201
Returns Inwards	2	
Carriage	16	
Stationery	1	
Electric Supplies Ltd		32
Warner and Sons	16	
Cash in hand	78	
Cash at Bank	245	
	£543	£543

Trading and Profit and Loss Account
for month ended 30th June, 19..

		£	£			£	£
Opening Stock		145		Sales		201	
Less Closing Stock		14		*Less* Returns		2	
							199
		131					
Gross Profit	c/d	68					
		£199					£199
Carriage		16		Gross Profit	b/d		68
Stationery		1					
Net Profit to Capital		51					
		£68					£68

Balance Sheet
as at 30th June, 19..

CLAIMS	£	£	ASSETS	£
Capital	310		Stock, 30th June	14
Add Net Profit	51		Debtors	16
	——		Cash at Bank	245
	361		Cash in hand	78
Less Drawings	40			
	——	321		
Creditors		32		
		£353		£353

For further details see solutions to Chapter 5, Exercise No. 3.

Chapter 10   Exercises

1 and **2**   See Example, pages 78 to 80 in textbook.

3   See pages 78 to 81.

4

	Journal			*Dr.*	*Cr.*
19 . .			£	£	£
May 31	Shop Fittings	2		1 200	
	Stock: Cutlery and Tools	3	6 000		
	Gardening Sundries		8 000		
				14 000	
	Cash at Bank	CB		2 600	
	Cash in hand	CB		190	
	Creditors: J. Smith	10			590
	Capital: J. Whitehouse	1			17 400
	Being assets, liabilities				
	and capital at this date			£17 990	£17 990

Purchases Book

19 . .		*Fol.*	*Totals*	*Cutlery and Tools*	*Garden-ing Sundries*
			£	£	£
June 2	J. Smith	10	780	780	
24	J. Smith	10	750	300	450
		3	£1 530	£1 080	£450

Sales Book

19 . .		Fol.	Totals	Cutlery and Tools	Garden- ing Sundries
			£	£	£
June 10	C. Welchman	11	420	160	260
15	B. Wells	12	240		240
		4	£660	£160	£500

Dr.   **Cash Book**   Cr.

19 . .			Cash £	Bank £	19 . .			Cash £	Bank £
June 1	Balances	J	190	2 600	June 12	Carriage	5	10	
8	Sales:				20	Advertising	6		50
	Cutlery	4		340	21	J. Smith	10		1 370
	Garden				21	Stationery	7	10	
	Sundries			630	21	Packing			
30	Sales:					Materials	8	20	
	Cutlery	4		860	30	Rent	9		300
	Garden				30	Balances	c/d	150	4 210
	Sundries			1 500					
			£190	£5 930				£190	£5 930
July 1	Balances	b/d	150	4 210					

LEDGER
Capital—J. Whitehouse[1]

19 . .			£	19 . .			£
June 30	Balance	c/d	18 230	June 1	Balance	J	17 400
				30	Net Profit	T	830
			£18 230				£18 230
				July 1	Balance	b/d	18 230

Shop Fittings[2]

19 . .			£	19 . .			£
June 1	Balance	J	1 200				

Stock[3]

Date	Particulars	Fol.	Totals £	Cutlery and Tools £	Gardening Sundries £	Date	Particulars	Fol.	Totals £	Cutlery and Tools £	Gardening Sundries £
19..						19..					
June 1	Balances	J	14 000	6 000	8 000	June 30	Trading A/c	T	14 000	6 000	8 000
June 30	Trading A/c	T	12 750	6 100	6 650						

Purchases[3]

Date	Particulars	Fol.	Totals £	Cutlery and Tools £	Gardening Sundries £	Date	Particulars	Fol.	Totals £	Cutlery and Tools £	Gardening Sundries £
19..						19..					
June 30	Goods	PDB	1 530	1 080	450	June 30	Trading A/c	T	1 530	1 080	450

Sales[4]

Date	Particulars	Fol.	Totals £	Cutlery and Tools £	Gardening Sundries £	Date	Particulars	Fol.	Totals £	Cutlery and Tools £	Gardening Sundries £
19..						19..					
June 30	Trading A/c	T	3 990	1 360	2 630	June 8	Cash	CB	970	340	630
						30	,, Goods	CB	2 360	860	1 500
						30		SDB	660	160	500
			£3 990	£1 360	£2 360				£3 990	£1 360	£2 630

Carriage[5]

19.. June 12	Cash	CB	£ 10	19.. June 30	Profit and Loss A/c	T	£ 10

Advertising[6]

19.. June 20	Cash	CB	£ 50	19.. June 30	Profit and Loss A/c	T	£ 50

Stationery[7]

19.. June 21	Cash	CB	£ 10	19.. June 30	Profit and Loss A/c	T	£ 10

Packing and Materials[8]

19.. June 21	Cash	CB	£ 20	June 30	Profit and Loss A/c	T	£ 20

Rent[9]

19.. June 30	Cash	CB	£ 300	19.. June 30	Profit and Loss A/c	T	£ 300

J. Smith[10]

19..			£	19..			£
June 21	Cash	CB	1 370	June 1	Balance	J	590
30	Balance	c/d	750	2	Purchases	PB	780
				24	,,	PB	750
			£2 120				£2 120
				July 1	Balance	b/d	750

C. Welchman[11]

19..			£	19..			£
June 10	Sales	SB	420				

B. Wells[12]

19..			£	19..			£
June 15	Sales	SB	240				

Trial Balance
30th June, 19..

	£	Dr. £	Cr. £
Capital			17 400
Shop Fittings		1 200	
Stock, 1st June, 19....			
Cutlery and Tools	6 000		
Gardening Sundries	8 000		
		14 000	
Purchases:			
Cutlery and Tools	1 080		
Gardening Sundries	450		
		1 530	
Sales:			
Cutlery and Tools	1 360		
Gardening Sundries	2 630		
			3 990
Packing Materials		20	
Carriage		10	
Advertising		50	
Stationery		10	
Rent		300	
J. Smith			750
C. Welchman		420	
B. Wells		240	
Cash in hand		150	
Cash at Bank		4 210	
		£22 140	£22 140

Trading and Profit and Loss Account
for month ended 30th June, 19..

	Totals £	Cutlery and Tools £	Gardening Sundries £
Opening Stocks, 1st June	14 000	6 000	8 000
Purchases	1 530	1 080	450
	15 530	7 080	8 450
Less Closing Stocks, 30th June	12 750	6 100	6 650
Cost of Sales	2 780	980	1 800
Gross Profit c/d	1 210	380	830
	3 990	1 360	2 630
Rent	300	100	200
Advertising	50	17	33
Carriage	10	4	6
Packing Materials	20	7	13
Stationery	10	4	6
Net Profit to Capital	820	248	572
	£1 210	£380	£830

	Totals £	Cutlery and Tools £	Gardening Sundries £
Sales	3 990	1 360	2 630
Gross Profit b/d	1 210	380	830
	£1 210	£380	£830

Alternative method

Trading and Profit and Loss Account
for month ended 30th June, 19.2

	Totals £	Cutlery and Tools £	Gardening Sundries £
Sales	3 990	1 360	2 630
Stocks, 1st June, 19.1	14 000	6 000	8 000
Purchases	1 530	1 080	450
	15 530	7 080	8 450
Less Stocks, 30th June, 19.2	12 750	6 100	6 650
Cost of Sales	2 780	980	1 800
Gross Profit (being excess of Sales over Cost of Sales)	1 210	380	830
Rent	300	100	200
Advertising	50	17	33
Carriage	10	4	6
Packing Materials	20	7	13
Stationery	10	4	6
	390	132	258
Net Profit transferred to Capital	820	248	572

If in this exercise there had been items in addition to Gross Profit on the credit side of the Profit and Loss Account, then the conventional ledger method would have been more convenient. But it is the Trading Account only which is usually analysed in order to show the Gross Profit of each department. The *total* Gross Profit is then carried down to the credit column of the Profit and Loss Account and the expense items are shown in the debit column as follows:

19 ..			£	£	£
Gross Profit:					
Cutlery and Tools	c/d	380			
Gardening Sundries		830			
					1 210
Less Expenditure:					
Rent				300	
Advertising				50	
Carriage				10	
Packing Materials				20	
Stationery				10	
					390
Net Profit transferred to Capital					£820

Balance Sheet
as at 30th June, 19..

CLAIMS	£	£		£	£	ASSETS
Capital				*Fixed Assets*		
J. Whitehouse	17 400			Shop Fittings		1 200
Add Net Profit	820			*Current Assets*		
		18 220		Stocks, 30th June:		
Current Liabilities				Cutlery and		
Creditors		750		Tools	6 100	
				Gardening		
				Sundries	6 650	
						12 750
				Debtors	660	
				Cash at Bank	4 210	
				Cash in hand	150	
						17 770
		£18 970				£18 970

5

Gross Profit	(A) 42 200 (B) 28 900	= 71 100
Net Profit	(A) 23 354 (B) 16 336	= 39 690
Balance Sheet totals		= 188 200

6

Gross Profit	(A) 17 000 (B) 11 300 (C) 27 400	= 55 700
Net Profit	(A) 12 188 (B) 8 092 (C) 19 380	= 39 660
Balance Sheet totals		= 75 700

Chapter 11   Exercises

1 (a) See page 87 of textbook.

1 (b)

Cash Book

Dr.

19.. Feb.	Particulars		Disct. Allowed £	Cash £	Bank £
1	Balance			270·00	1 100·00
2	F. Johnson		20·00	230·00	
3	A. Bowman			20·00	
4	W. Winter				350·00
5	A. Crowe		2·50	47·50	
6	Sales			120·00	
6	Cash	C			300·00
			£22·50	£687·50	£1 750·00
Feb. 7	Balances	b/d		317·50	1 255·00

Cr.

19.. Feb.	Particulars		Disct. Recd. £	Cash £	Bank £
3	R. Shipley		5·00	30·00	195·00
4	L. Patterson				
4	Expenses			30·00	
5	Postage Stamps			10·00	
6	J. Williams		20·00		300·00
6	Bank	C		300·00	
6	Balances	c/d		317·50	1 255·00
			£25·00	£687·50	£1 750·00

2

Cash Book Balances: Bank—£189·45
                Cash—£12·00
Discounts Allowed total £1.
Discounts Received total £4·45.

3

LEDGER (Extract)
R. Lee

19 . . Feb. 6	Cash Discount		£ 47·50 2·50	19 . . Feb. 1	Balance		£ 50·00
			£50·00				£50·00

L. Peacock

19 . . Feb. 2 8	Sales ,,		£ 30·00 300·00	19 . . Feb. 9 9 16	Cash Discount Balance	 c/d	£ 28·00 2·00 300·00
			£330·00				£330·00
Feb. 17	Balance	b/d	300·00				

Trial Balance
16th February, 19 . .

	£	£
Capital		941·00
Drawings	30·00	
Fixtures and Fittings	72·00	
Motor Van	375·00	
Purchases	81·00	
Sales		352·00
Returns Outwards		32·40
Stock	250·00	
Postages	6·00	
Expenses	4·00	
Discounts Allowed	2·00	
Discounts Received		2·50
Austins Ltd		375·00
T. Gelling		79·60
L. Peacock	300·00	
Cash in hand	17·00	
Cash at Bank	645·50	
	£1 782·50	£1 782·50

Trading and Profit and Loss Account
for 16 days ended 16th February, 19..

		£	£			£
Opening Stock			250·00	Sales		352·00
Purchases		81·00				
Less Returns		32·40				
			48·60			
			298·60			
Less Closing Stock			46·00			
			252·60			
Gross Profit	c/d		99·40			
			£352·00			£352·00
				Gross Profit	b/d	99·40
Postages			6·00	Discounts Received		2·50
Expenses			4·00			
Discounts Allowed			2·00			
Net Profit to Capital			89·90			
			£101·90			£101·90

Balance Sheet
as at 16th February, 19..

CLAIMS	£	£	ASSETS	£	£
Capital	941·00		*Fixed Assets*		
Add Net Profit	89·90		Fixtures and		
			Fittings	72·00	
	1 030·90		Motor Van	375·00	
Less Drawings	30·00				447·00
		1 000·90			
Current Liabilities			*Current Assets*		
Creditors		454·60	Stock,		
			16th February	46·00	
			Debtors	300·00	
			Cash at Bank	645·50	
			Cash in hand	17·00	
					1 008·50
		£1 455·50			£1 455·50

4   Cash Balance £32; Bank Balance £210; Trial Balance totals £2 994.

5   Cash Balance £60; Bank Balance £440; Trial Balance totals £6 080; Gross Profit £340; No Profit or Loss; Balance Sheet totals £4 780.

K. Brown

The particulars given in the Particulars columns also indicate
the double entry accounts

19..			£	19..			£
Jan. 15	Returns Outwards	ROB	20	Jan. 1	Balance b/d from		
20	Cash	CB	100		debit side of		
					previous period.		
					Amount owing		
Feb. 10	Cash	CB	323		to Brown		120
10	Discount Received	T	17	10	Goods—Purchases		
					from Brown on		
					Credit	PB	340
			£460				£460

Chapter 12   Exercises

1

	Journal	Dr.	Cr.
19..		£	£
Jan. 14	Motor Vans	6 750	
	London Motor Co.		6 750
	Purchase of delivery van		
17	Office Furniture	450	
	Shoreditch Cabinet Co.		450
	Purchase of office desk		
25	Office Machinery	400	
	British Typewriter Co.		400
	Purchase of typewriter		
30	Furniture and Fittings	1 650	
	Mint and Co.		1 650
	Purchase of two showcases		
	and other fittings		

2

	Journal	Dr.	Cr.
19..		£	£
Feb. 2	Warehouse and Showrooms	10 000	
	Freehold Properties Co.		10 000
	Purchase of warehouse and showrooms		
6	Car Mart Auction Co.	150	
	Motor Vans		150
	Sale of delivery van		
8	Drawings: A. Bentley	20	
	Purchases		20
	Sideboard taken from stock for own use		
10	Office Machinery	50	
	Furniture Supplies Co.		50
	Purchase of cash register		
12	Motor Vans	5 000	
	City Motor Co.		5 000
	Purchase of delivery van		

3

	Journal	Dr.	Cr.
19..		£	£
Jan. 1	Cash in hand	27	
	Cash at Bank	230	
	Debtors: Williams and Co.	20	
	Wilson and Sons	35	
	Stock	750	
	Creditors: J. Bones		130
	T. Smith		150
	Capital		782
	Being Assets and Claims at this date	£1 062	£1 062

4

	Journal		Dr.	Cr.
19..			£	£
	Shop Fittings	2	60	
	Office Furniture	4	50	
	Delivery Bicycle	3	10	
	Stock	5	800	
	Debtor: Brown and Co.	6	204	
	Cash at Bank	CB	321	
	Cash in hand	CB	10	
	Creditors: J. Westerby	7		87
	R. Easter	8		31
	B. Groombridge	9		8
	Capital (Excess of assets over			
	liabilities)	1		1 329
	Being Assets and Claims		£1 455	£1 455

Cash Book

Dr.			Cash £	Bank £	Cr.			Cash £	Bank £
19..	Balance	J	10	321	19..				

LEDGER

Capital[1]

19..			£	19..			£
					Balance	J	1 329

Shop Fitting[2]

19..			£	19..			£
	Balance	J	60				

Delivery Bicycle[3]

19..	Balance	J	£ 10	19..			£

Office Furniture[4]

19..	Balance	J	£ 50	19..			£

Stock[5]

19..	Balance	J	£ 800	19..			£

Brown and Co.[6]

19..	Balance	J	£ 204	19..			£

J. Westerby[7]

19..			£	19..	Balance	J	£ 87

R. Easter[8]

19..			£	19..	Balance	J	£ 31

B. Groombridge[9]

19..			£	19..	Balance	J	£ 8

5

Journal	Dr.	Cr.
19..	£	£
Jan. 1 Cash in hand	30	
Cash at Bank	320	
Debtors: J. Neill	150	
R. Firth	380	
N. Tyson	20	
Stock	530	
Furniture and Fittings	110	
Creditors: R. Jones		240
T. Lewis		120
Capital		1 180
Being Assets and Claims at this date	£1 540	£1 540

6

Trial Balance
17th January, 19..

	Dr.	Cr.
	£	£
Cash in hand	13	
Cash at Bank	201	
Capital		2 230
Purchases	50	
Sales		130
Stock	750	
Petrol and Oil	7	
Premises	1 200	
Shop Fittings	152	
Delivery Van	120	
B. Brown		33
Cabinet Makers Co. Ltd.		100
	£2 493	£2 493

Gross Profit £100; Net Profit £93; Balance Sheet totals £2 456.

7

Cash Balance £100; Bank Balance £5 180; Trial Balance totals £14 580; Gross Profit £250; Net Loss £50; Balance Sheet totals £13 530; Capital 1st July £13 830.

8

19 . .	Journal	Dr.	Cr.
		£	£
Sept. 2	B. Clark	20	
	J. B. Clarkson		20
	Correction of item wrongly posted to Clarkson's Account		
10	Sales	10	
	Office Furniture		10
	Sale of desk posted to Sales Account in error		
13	Office Furniture	36	
	Purchases		36
	Purchase of desk posted to Purchases in error		
17	R. Williamson and Son	75	
	R. Wilkinson and Co.		75
	Purchase posted to R. Williamson and Son in error		

9

19 . .	Journal	Dr.	Cr.
		£	£
July 3	R. Levy	50	
	R. Lewis		50
	Correction of wrong posting		
28	R. Jones	25	
	R. B. Jones and Co.		25
	Correction of wrong posting		
31	Office Machinery	15	
	Purchases		15
	Correction of wrong posting to Purchases		
Aug. 6	B. Watson	10	
	B. Watkinson		10
	Correction of wrong posting		

10

19 . .	Journal	Dr.	Cr.
		£	£
Dec. 31	Trading Account	1 600	
	Purchases		1 600
	Balance transferred		
31	Sales	2 590	
	Trading Account		2 590
	Balance transferred		
31	Trading Account	300	
	Stock		300
	Balance transferred		
31	Profit and Loss Account	*317	
	Wages		120
	Expenses		47
	Rent		150
	Balances transferred		
		£317	£317
Dec. 31	Stock	400	
	Trading Account		400
	Closing stock transferred		

*It would, of course, be in order to make separate entries (instead of a composite as shown), if preferred.

11

	Journal			Dr.	Cr.
19 . . Aug. 31	Suspense Account			30	
	A. Brown				20
	Sales				10
	Correction of error				
31	Rent			25	
	Suspense Account				25
	Correction of error				

LEDGER
Suspense Account

19 . . Aug. 31 31	A. Brown Sales		£ 20 10	19 . . Aug. 31 31	Rent Trial Balance Error	£ 25 5
			£30			£30

12

	Journal			Dr.	Cr.
19 . . Feb. 1				£ 18	£
	P. Dawson				
	F. Dawson and Co.				18
	Cheque posted to P. Dawson in error				
1	Sales Account			10	
	Returns Outwards Account				10
	Entry in wrong Day Book (which ultimately affected the account) corrected				
1	Legal Expenses			5	
	G. Law				5
	Correction of entry in wrong account				

13

	Journal			Dr.	Cr.
19 . . Dec. 1				£ 5	£
	G. Sykes				
	Commission				5
	5% commission on £100				
31	Business Premises			119	
	Wages				56
	Purchases				63
	Amounts paid in connection with extension of business premises and wrongly entered in Wages and Purchases Accounts, respectively				
31	Suspense Account			10	
	Sales Returns				5
	Purchases Returns				5
	Correction of error				

$$\frac{\text{Profit before Commission}}{\text{Profit after Commission}} = \frac{100}{110}$$

$\frac{100}{110} \times 1100 = £1\,000 = $ Profit after payment of Commission

Chapter 13   Exercises

1 See pages 109–111 in textbook.

2

Sales Ledger Control Account

19..			£	19..			£
May 1	Balance	b/d	4 607	May 31	Returns and		
31	Sales		5 291		Allowances		342
					Cash		3 996
					Discounts		197
					Bad Debts		47
					Balance	c/d	5 316
			£9 898				£9 898
June 1	Balance	b/d	5 316				

3

Bought Ledger Control Account

19..			£	19..			£
May 31	Returns and			May 1	Balance	b/d	8 409
	Allowances		243		Purchases		7 308
	Cash		6 504				
	Discounts		292				
	Balance	c/d	8 678				
			£15 717				£15 717
				June 1	Balance	b/d	8 678

4

Bought Ledger Control Account

19..			£	19..			£
Jan. 1	Balance	b/d	58	Jan. 1	Balance	b/d	983
31	Returns			31	Purchases		2 938
	Outwards		100	31	Balance	c/d	83
	Cash		2 659				
	Discounts						
	Received		56				
	Sales Ledger	T	50				
	Balance	c/d	1 081				
			£4 004				£4 004
Feb. 1	Balance	b/d	83	Feb. 1	Balance	b/d	1 081

Sales Ledger Control Account

19..			£	19..			£
Jan. 1	Balance	b/d	3 694	Jan. 1	Balance	b/d	149
31	Sales		8 523	31	Returns		
	Balance	c/d	49		Inwards		193
					Cash		6 954
					Discounts		
					Allowed		80
					Bought		
					Ledger	T	50
					Bad Debts		25
					Balance	c/d	4 815
			£12 266				£12 266
Feb. 1	Balance	b/d	4 815	Feb. 1	Balance	b/d	49

5

	Journal	*Dr.*	*Cr.*
19..		£	£
	R. Tyler: Purchases Ledger	137	
	R. Tyler: Sales Ledger		137
	Transfer of balance from (i) Sales to		
	(ii) Purchases Ledger, closing the account		
	in (i) and reducing the balance in (ii)		
	from £207 to £70		

This item would be posted to the debit side of R. Tyler's Account in the Bought Ledger and to the credit side of his account in the Sales Ledger.

This is sometimes called a 'contra' entry and (if a journal entry is not made) the letter 'C' (for contra) is inserted in the respective folio columns of the two ledgers.

6 (*a*)

Sales Ledger Control Account

19..			£	19..				£
Oct. 1	Balance	b/d	10 461	Oct. 1	Balance	b/d		81
31	Sales		12 484	31	Returns			
	Balance	c/d	131		Inwards			140
					Cash			11 058
					Discounts			
					Allowed			582
					Bought			
					Ledger	C		104
					Balance	c/d		11 111
			£23 076					£23 076
Nov. 1	Balance	b/d	11 111	Nov. 1	Balance	b/d		131

6 (*b*)

		£			
1. (i) Dr. Sales Account		270	2.	(i) No change	
(ii) Cr. F. Ames		6		(ii) ,, ,,	
(iii) Dr. Discount Account		10		(iii) Increase Discounts on	
				credit side £10	
(iv) Dr. J. Braggs		10		(iv) No change	
(v) Cr. W. Carr		9		(v) ,, ,,	

Chapter 14   Exercises

1

Trial Balance
17th March, 19..	*Dr.*	*Cr.*
	£	£
Capital		6 000
Freehold Premises	3 600	
Fixtures and Fittings	186	
Scales and Cash Register	72	
Packing Materials	13	
Wages	3	
Purchases and Sales	1 500	258
National Stores		1 200
Hudson and Co.		300
Cash at Bank	2 339	
Cash in hand	45	
	£7 758	£7 758

Trading and Profit and Loss Account
for 17 days ended 17th March, 19. .

19..			£	19..			£
	Purchases		1 500		Sales		258
	Less Closing Stock		1 305				
			195				
	Gross Profit	c/d	63				
			£258				£258
	Wages		3		Gross Profit	b/d	63
	Packing Materials		13				
	Net Profit to Capital		47				
			£63				£63

Balance Sheet
as at 17th March, 19. .

CLAIMS	£	£	ASSETS	£	£
Capital:			*Fixed Assets:*		
J. Herbertson	6 000		Freehold Premises	3 600	
Add Net Profit	47		Fixtures and Fittings	186	
		6 047	Scales and Cash Register	72	
Current Liabilities:					3 858
Creditors		1 500	*Current Assets:*		
			Stock, 17th March	1 305	
			Cash at Bank	2 339	
			Cash in hand	45	
					3 689
		£7 547			£7 547

2 to 5	2	3	4	5
	£	£	£	£
Cash Balance	5	100		
Bank Balance	145	1 820		
Trial Balance totals	1 110	39 270		
Gross Profit	164	9 800	9 700	13 380
Net Profit	134	3 950	3 890	4 000
Balance Sheet totals	774	16 220	15 400	13 210

6 See page 116 of textbook.

7

Driving School	*Capital*	*Revenue*
	Freehold Garage and Office	Petrol and Oil
		Rates
	Cars	Tyres and Spares
	Servicing Equipment	Salaries and Wages
		Tax and Insurance
Bus Operator	Freehold Premises	Fuel
	Buses	Tax and Insurance
	Plant	Salaries and Wages
		Rates
Wholesale Grocery and Provision Merchants	Freehold Warehouse	Salaries and Wages
	Fixtures and Fittings	Heat and Light
	Winches	Rates
	Trolleys	Stocks
	Scales	Packing Materials

8

  (i) Capital.
 (ii) Revenue.
(iii) Capital.
 (iv) Revenue.
  (v) Revenue.

9

Balance Sheet of T. S. Appleby
as at 31st May, 19. .

CLAIMS	£	£	ASSETS	£	£	£
Capital:			*Fixed Assets:*			
Being the excess of			Machinery		2 000	
Assets over			Furniture and			
Liabilities and due			Fittings		350	
to T. S. Appleby		4 000	Motor Vans		1 200	
						3 550
Loan Accounts:			*Current Assets:*			
V. Appleby	750		Stock	1 340		
T. Garth and Sons	600		Debtors	2 376		
			Cash in hand	24		
		1 350			3 740	
			Current Liabilities:			
			Creditors	1 850		
			Bank Overdraft	90		
					1 940	
			Working Capital			1 800
Capital Employed		£5 350	Net Value of Assets			£5 350

10

	£
(i) Total Fixed Assets	2 010
(ii) Total Current Assets	9 750
(iii) Total Current Liabilities	4 310
(iv) Working Capital	5 440
(v) Net Book Value of Assets	7 450
(iv) Capital Employed	7 450

Chapter 15

The Worked Example is a comprehensive exercise illustrating all the principles expounded up to and including Chapter 14. It will be found very useful as a reference to details of the basic principles of bookkeeping.

Chapter 16   Exercises

1 to 7   The answers are clearly stated in Chapter 16.

Chapter 17   Exercises

1   Rule the necessary columns in accordance with the example given on page 145. Total payments £5·26; Balance c/d £4·74.

2   (*a*) See page 144.

2(*b*)

Receipts	Cash Book Folio	Date	Particulars		Total Payments	Postage & Telegrams	Carriage	Stationery
£					£	£	£	£
15·00		Jan. 4	Balance					
		4	Postage Stamps		1·50	1·50		
		5	Stationery		3·50			3·50
		5	Carriage		0·85		0·85	
		6	Postage Stamps		1·25	1·25		
		8	Stationery		1·50			1·50
			Total		8·60	£2·75	£0·85	£5·00
8·60		8	Cash					
		10	Balance	c/d	15·00			
£23·00					£23·60			
15·00		11	Balance	b/d				

3   July 6. Balance c/d £0·02.

4

Jan. 31	Balance c/d £5·23: *Totals*—Postages and Telegrams	£ 2·23
	Office Expenses	4·17
	Purchases of Goods for Resale	8·37
		14·77
	Balance c/d	5·23
		£20·00

5 Feb. 28. Balance c/d £6·40.
      28. Amount added to Balance (Imprest) £8·60.

6 Jan. 8. Total Expenditure £40·72; Balance c/d £9·28.

Chapter 18   Exercises

1

Bank Reconciliation Statement
31st December, 19 . .

	£
Bank Statement Balance	293
Less Cheques drawn and not yet presented	54
	239
Add Cheques paid in and not yet credited	72
Cash Book Balance	£311

2

Bank Reconciliation Statement
31st December, 19 . .

	£
Bank Statement Balance	142
Less Cheques drawn and not yet presented	32
	110
Add Cheques paid in and not yet credited	104
Cash Book Balance	£214

3

Bank Reconciliation Statement
31st December, 19 . .

	£	£
Cash Book Balance		327·95
Add Cheques drawn and not yet presented		32·94
		360·89
Less Cheques paid in and not yet shown on the Statement	616·40	
Less Bank Interest	12·38	
		628·78
Bank Overdraft as per Bank Statement		£267·89

4

Bank Reconciliation Statement
30th June, 19 . .

		£
Bank Statement Balance		689·55
Add Cheques paid in and not yet credited		76·45
Add Bank charges not in cash book		5·50
Add Standing Order payment not in cash book		5·00
		776·50
Less Cheque drawn and not yet presented	284·35	
Less Dividends received not in cash book	98·75	
		383·10
Cash book balance		£393·40

Dr.				Cash Book			Cr.
19 . .			£	19 . .			£
June 30	Balance		393·40	June 30	Bank Charges		5·50
	Dividends		98·75		Trade Protection		
					Society S/O		5·00
					Balance	c/d	481·65
			£492·15				£492·15
July 1	Balance	b/d	481·65				

5

Dr.			Cash Book			Cr.
19..		£	19..			£
May 31	Balance	370·40	May 31	Insurance (Fire)		
	Interest:			Premium S/O	c/d	12·85
	Westshire			Balance		394·30
	C.C.	36·75				
		£407·15				£407·15
June 1	Balance	b/d 394·30				

Bank Reconciliation Statement
31st May, 19..

	£
Bank Statement Balance	409·50
Less Cheques drawn and not yet presented	100·57
	308·93
Add Cheque paid in and not yet credited	85·37
Cash Book Balance	£394·30

Chapter 19   Exercises

1   Cash Balance £30; Bank Overdraft £170; Trial Balance totals £1 816·50; Gross Profit £54; Net Profit £33; Balance Sheet totals £1 671.

2

LEDGER (Extract)
6% Bank Loan

19..			£	19..			£
				June 15	Cash		3 000

Interest on Loan

19..			£	19..			£
June 30	Cash	CB	7	June 30	Profit and Loss A/c	T	7

Trial Balance

30th June, 19..	Dr.	Cr.
	£	£
Capital		2 595
Machinery	3 800	
Fixtures and Fittings	150	
Stock, June 15th	1 500	
Sales		133
Expenses	20	
Carriage	10	
Interest on Loan	7	
C. Smart	50	
R. Sharp	40	
J. Cutler		70
Mint and Co.		150
Bank Loan Account		3 000
Cash at Bank	356	
Cash in hand	15	
	£5 948	£5 948

Gross Profit £33; Net Loss £4.

Balance Sheet
as at 30th June, 19..

CLAIMS	£	£	ASSETS	£	£
Capital	2 595		*Fixed Assets*		
Less Net Loss	4		Machinery	3 800	
		2 591	Fixtures and		
6% Bank Loan		3 000	Fittings	150	
					3 950
Current Liabilities			*Current Assets*		
Creditors:			Stock, 30th June	1 400	
Trade	70		Debtors	90	
Fixtures and			Cash at Bank	356	
Fittings A/c	150		Cash in hand	15	
		220			1 861
		£5 811			£5 811

3 Gross Profit £13 360; Net Profit £6 300; Balance Sheet total £13 050.

4
(*a*) To check the arithmetical accuracy of the accounts during a given period. See also Chapter 6, pages 43–47.
(*b*) To ascertain the Gross Profit. See also Chapter 3, pages 13 and 14.
(*c*) To ascertain the Net Profit. See also Chapter 3, pages 15 and 16.
(*d*) To summarise the financial position of the business at a given moment in time. See also Chapter 3, pages 18 and 19.

5

Trial Balance 31st January, 19..	Dr.	Cr.
	£	£
Capital: J. Abbots		6 567·00
Loan Account: S. Roberts		4 200·00
Leasehold Premises	5 950·00	
Fixtures and Fittings	757·00	
Stock, 1st January	4 120·000	
Purchases and Sales	1 360·00	60·00
Returns Outwards		36·00
Expenses	50·00	
Interest on Loan	126·00	
Discounts Allowed	9·50	
J. Gibbs		500·00
T. Orrett		96·00
A. Robbins		144·00
B. Fearn & Co. Ltd.		220·00
Music Centres Ltd.		960·00
T. Tomkins	256·00	
Cash in hand	51·00	
Cash at Bank	103·50	
	£12 783·00	£12 783·00

Chapter 20   Exercises

1

Journal		Dr.	Cr.
19.. Dec. 31	Profit and Loss Account	£ 450	£
	Provisions for Bad Debts		
	Provision for Bad Debts		450

Provisions for Bad Debts

19..		£	19.. Dec. 31	Profit and Loss A/c		£ 450

Profit and Loss Account

19.. Dec. 31	Provision for Bad Debts	£ 450	19..		£

Balance Sheet

CLAIMS	£	£	ASSETS	£	£
			Debtors	5 000	
			Less Provision for		
			Bad Debts	450	
					4 550

2

	Journal	*Dr.*	*Cr.*
19..		£	£
Dec. 31	Profit and Loss Account	137·50	
	Provision for Bad Debts		137·50
	Provision of 5% on Debtors at this date		

Continue as in **1.**

3

Journal
Similar to **2.**

4

	Journal	*Dr.*	*Cr.*
19..		£	£
Dec. 31	Profit and Loss Account	60	
	Provision for Bad Debts		60
	An increase to maintain provision of		
	5% on Debtors		

Provision for Bad Debts

19..			£	19..			£
Dec. 31	Balance	c/d	210	Jan. 1	Balance		150
				Dec. 31	Profit and		60
					Loss A/c		
			£210				£210
				Jan. 1	Balance	b/d	210

Profit and Loss Account

19..			£	19..			£
Dec. 31	Provision for						
	Bad Debts		60				

Balance Sheet
(Assets side)

CLAIMS	£	£	ASSETS	£	£
			Debtors	4 200	
			Less Provision for		
			Bad Debts	210	
					3 990

5 and **6**   Both are similar to **4.**
The amounts required to raise the respective provisions being: **5** = £35; **6** = £45.

7

	Journal			Dr.		Cr.
19..				£		£
Dec. 31	Provision for Bad Debts			60		
	Profit and Loss Account					60
	Excess written back to maintain					
	Provision at 5% on Debtors					

Provision for Bad Debts

19..			£	19..			£
Dec. 31	Profit and			Jan. 1	Balance	b/d	360
	Loss A/c		60				
	Balance	c/d	300				
			£360				£360
				Jan. 1	Balance	b/d	300

Profit and Loss Account

19..			£	19..			£
				Dec. 31	Provision for		60
					Bad Debts		

8 and **9**   Both similar to **7.** The excess to be written back (*i.e.* the decrease) in each case being: **8** = £130; **9** = £120.

10

Balance Sheet

Claims		£	£	Assets	£	£
				Debtors	12 500·00	
				Less Provision for Bad Debts	625·00	
					11 875·00	
				Less Provision for Discounts	296·87½	
						11 578·12½

11

Journal			Dr.	Cr.
1.. Dec. 31	Profit and Loss Account		£ 400	£
	Provision for Bad Debts			400
	Provision of 5% on Debtors (£8 000)			
31	Profit and Loss Account		190	
	Provision for Discounts on Debtors			190
	Provision of 2½% on Debtors (£8 000 − £400 = £7 600)			

Provision for Discounts on Debtors

19..			£	19.. Dec. 31	Profit and Loss A/c		£ 190

Provision for Bad Debts

19..			£	19.. Dec. 31	Profit and Loss A/c		£ 400

Profit and Loss Account

19.. Dec. 31	Provision for Bad Debts		£ 400	19..			£
	Provision for Discounts on Debtors		190				

Balance Sheet
(Assets side)

CLAIMS	£	£	ASSETS	£	£
			Debtors	8 000	
			Less Provision for		
			Bad Debts	400	
				7 600	
			Less Provision for		
			Discounts	190	
					7 410

12 Similar to **11.**

13

	Journal			Dr.	Cr.
19 . .				£	£
Dec. 31	Provision for Discounts on Creditors			125	
	Profit and Loss Account				125
	Provision of 2½% Cash Discount on				
	Creditors				

Provision for Discounts on Creditors

19 . .			£	19 . .			£
Dec. 31	Profit and						
	Loss A/c		125				

Profit and Loss Account

19 . .			£	19 . .	19 . .		
				Dec. 31	Provision		
					for		
					Discounts		
					on Creditors		125

Balance Sheet
(Claims side)

CLAIMS	£	£	ASSETS	£	£
Creditors	5 000				
Less Provision for					
Discounts	125				
		4 875			

14 Similar to above examples.

Balance Sheet
(Extract)

CLAIMS	£	£	ASSETS	£	£
Creditors	5 000·00		Debtors	7 000·00	
Less Provision for			*Less* Provision for		
Discounts	125·00		Bad Debts	350·00	
		4 875·00		6 650·00	
			Less Provision for		
			Discounts	166·25	
					6 483·75

15

Journal			Dr.	Cr.
19 . .			£	£
Mar. 23	Bad Debts		65·45	
	A. Sharp			65·45
	Balance of Debts written off on bankruptcy			

Cash Book

19 . .		£	19 . .		£
Feb. 8	A. Sharp 1st Dividend of £0·10 in £ on £77	7·70			
Mar. 23	A. Sharp 2nd Dividend of £0·05 in £ on £77	3·85			

Bad Debts

19 . .		£	19 . .		£
Mar. 23	A. Sharp	65·45			

A. Sharp

19 . .			£	19 . .		£
Jan. 1	Balance	b/d	77·00	Feb. 8	Cash 1st Dividend	7·70
				Mar. 23	Cash 2nd and Final Dividend	3·85
				23	Bad Debts	65·45
			£77·00			£77·00

Chapter 21 *Exercises*

1

Insurance

19.. Dec. 31	Balance		£ 600	19.. Dec. 31	Profit and Loss A/c		£ 450
				31	Balance: Amount Prepaid	c/d	150
			£600				£600
Jan. 1	Balance	b/d	150				

Rates

19.. Dec. 31	Balance		£ 3 000	19.. Dec. 31	Profit and Loss A/c		£ 2 250
				31	Balance: Amount Prepaid	c/d	750
			£3 000				£3 000
Jan. 1	Balance	b/d	750				

Balance Sheet

	Assets *Payments in Advance*	£	£
	Insurance	150	
	Rates	750	
		—	900

2

Rent

19.. Dec. 31	Balance		£ 7 500	19.. Dec. 31	Profit and Loss A/c		£ 10 000
31	Balance: Amount due	c/d	2 500				
			£10 000				£10 000
				Jan. 1	Balance	b/d	2 500

Similar to this account are the items Wages, Salaries, and Interest.
Similar to **1** are the items Rates, Insurance, Advertising.

3

Rent

19..			£	19..			£
Dec. 31	Balance		3 000	Dec. 31	Profit and		
31	Balance:				Loss A/c		4 000
	Amount due	c/d	1 000				
			£4 000				£4 000
				Jan. 1	Balance	b/d	1 000

Wages

19..			£	19..			£
Dec. 31	Balance		48 000	Dec. 31	Profit and		
31	Balance:				Loss A/c		48 500
	Wages due	c/d	500				
			£48 500				£48 500
				Jan. 1	Balance	b/d	500

Balance Sheet

CLAIMS	£	£
Current Liabilities		
Rent due	1 000	
Wages accrued	500	
	———	1 500

4

Rent Receivable

19..			£	19..			£
Dec. 31	Profit and			Mar. 25	Cash		120
	Loss A/c		480	June 24	,,		120
				Sept. 29	,,		120
				Dec. 31	Balance:		
					Rent due	c/d	120
			£480				£480
Jan. 1	Balance	b/d	120				

5

	Journal	Dr.	Cr.
19..		£	£
	(a) Bad Debts	1 010·00	
	A		550·00
	B		190·00
	C		270·00
	Amounts due from sundry debtors written off as irrecoverable		
	(b) Profit and Loss Account	10 000·00	
	General Reserve		10 000·00
	Amount allocated to General Reserve		
	(c) Furniture and Fittings	450·00	
	Office Expenses		450·00
	Amount debited to Office Expenses in error		
	(d) Loan Account 'D'	62·50	
	Interest on Loan Account		62·50
	Interest at 5% per annum for three months		

6

Trading and Profit and Loss Account
for year ended 31st December, 19..

	£	Total £	Home £	Export £			Total £	Home £	Export £
Stock, 1st Jan.		5 591	2 962	2 629	Sales		53 441	28 027	25 414
Purchases		47 293	24 710	22 583	Stock		5 320	2 721	2 599
Gross Profit	c/d	5 877	3 076	2 801					
		£58 761	£30 748	£28 013			£58 761	£30 748	£28 013
Advertising		927	512	415	Gross				
Carriage		261	261		Profit	b/d	5 877	3 076	2 801
Freight		598		598					
Heat and Light		70	35	35					
Office Expenses		654	327	327					
Rates		120	60	60					
Provision for Bad Debts		173	173						
Salaries		1 524	726	798					
Commission	520								
Unpaid and Due	40								
		560	560						
Depreciation: Office Furniture		30	15	15					
Net Profit to Capital		960	407	553					
		£5 877	£3 076	£2 801			£5 877	£3 076	£2 801

Alternative method

Trading and Profit and Loss Account
for year ended 31st December, 19 . .

	£	Total £ £53 441	Home £ £28 027	Export £ £25 414
Sales		£53 441	£28 027	£25 414
Stock, 1st January		5 591	2 962	2 629
Purchases		47 293	24 710	22 583
		52 884	27 672	25 212
Less Stock, 31st December		5 320	2 721	2 599
Cost of Goods Sold		47 564	24 951	22 613
Gross Profit		£5 877	£3 076	£2 801
Advertising		927	512	415
Carriage		261	261	
Freight		598		598
Heat and Light		70	35	35
Office Expenses		654	327	327
Rates		120	60	60
Provision for Bad Debts		173	173	
Salaries		1 524	726	798
Commission	520			
Unpaid and Due	40			
		560	560	
Depreciation: Office Furniture		30	15	15
		4 917	2 669	2 248
Net Profit to Capital		960	407	553

See Chapter 10, Exercise No. 4 for additional instructions on the above.

Balance Sheet

as at 31st December, 19..

CLAIMS	£	£	ASSETS	£	£	£
Capital	12 382		*Fixed Assets*			
Add Net Profit:			Freehold Premises		3 500	
Home	407		Office Furniture	600		
Exports	553		*Less* Depreciation	30		
	— 960				— 570	
						— 4 070
	13 342		*Current Assets*			
Less Drawings	840		Stock, 31st Dec.			
	—	12 502	Home	2 721		
			Export	2 599		
Current Liabilities					— 5 320	
Creditors	3 756		Debtors	5 325		
Commission			*Less* Provision for			
unpaid	40		Bad Debts	273		
	—	3 796			— 5 052	
			Cash at Bank		1 786	
			Cash in hand		70	
					—	12 228
		£16 298				£16 298

Chapter 22   Exercises

1

Plant and Machinery

19..			£	19..			£
Jan. 1	Balance	b/d	40 000·00	Dec. 31	Depreciation	J	4 000·00
					Balance	c/d	36 000·00
			£40 000·00				£40 000·00
19.1				19.1			
Jan. 1	Balance	b/d	36 000·00	Dec. 31	Depreciation	J	3 600·00
					Balance	c/d	32 400·00
			£36 000·00				£36 000·00
19.2				19.2			
Jan. 1	Balance	b/d	32 400·00	Dec. 31	Depreciation	J	3 240·00
					Balance	c/d	29 160·00
			£32 400·00				£32 400·00
19.3							
Jan. 1	Balance	b/d	29 160·00				

Office Furniture

19.. Jan. 1	Balance	b/d	£ 4 000·00	19.. Dec. 31	Depreciation Balance	J c/d	£ 200·00 3 800·00
			£4 000·00				£4 000·00
19.1 Jan. 1	Balance	b/d	3 800·00	19.1 Dec. 31	Depreciation Balance	J c/d	190·00 3 610·00
			£3 800·00				£3 800·00
19.2 Jan. 1	Balance	b/d	3 610·00	19.2 Dec. 31	Depreciation Balance	J c/d	180·50 3 429·50
			£3 610·00				£3 610·00
19.3 Jan. 1	Balance	b/d	3 429·00				

Balance Sheet
As at 31st December, 19.1
(Extract from Assets side)

CLAIMS	£	£	ASSETS	£	£
			Plant and Machinery	40 000·00	
			Less Depreciation	4 000·00	
					36 000·00
			Office Furniture	4 000·00	
			Less Depreciation	20·00	
					3 800·00

Balance Sheet
As at 31st December, 19.2
(Extract from Assets side)

CLAIMS	£	£	ASSETS	£	£
			Plant and Machinery	40 000·00	
			Less Depreciation	7 600·00	
					32 400·00
			Office Furniture	4 000·00	
			Less Depreciation	390·00	
					3 610·00

Balance Sheet
As at 31st December, 19.3
(Extract from Assets side)

CLAIMS	£	£	ASSETS	£	£
			Plant and Machinery	40 000·00	
			Less Depreciation	10 840·00	
					29 160·00
			Office Furniture	4 000·00	
			Less Depreciation	570·50	
					3 429·50

2

Machinery

19.1			£	19.1				£
Jan. 1	Cash	CB	12 000	Dec. 31	Depreciation	J		1 000
					Balance	c/d		11 000
			£12 000					£12 000
19.2				19.2				
Jan. 1	Balance	b/d	11 000	Dec. 31	Depreciation	J		1 000
					Balance	c/d		10 000
			£11 000					£11 000
19.3				19.3				
Jan. 1	Balance	b/d	10 000	Dec. 31	Depreciation	J		1 000
					Balance	c/d		9 000
			£10 000					£10 000
19.4								
Jan. 1	Balance	b/d	9 000					

Depreciation

19.1			£	19.1		£
Dec. 31	Machinery	J	1 000	Dec. 31	Profit and Loss A/c	1 000
19.2				19.2		
Dec. 31	Machinery	J	1 000	Dec. 31	Profit and Loss A/c	1 000
19.3				19.3		
Dec. 31	Machinery	J	1 000	Dec. 31	Profit and Loss A/c	1 000

3 For Balance Sheet purposes, Fixed Assets should be valued at cost or current (book) value, depending on the nature of the asset, less depreciation. The annual charge for depreciation of the motor lorry is

$$\frac{£45\,000 - £2\,500}{7} = £6\,071$$

An additional annual charge should be made to provide for the increase in the replacement cost: $\dfrac{£5\,000}{7} = £714$.

This sum should be credited to a Reserve Account.

4

Electric Generator Plant

19..			£	19..			£
Jan. 1	Cash	CB	25 000	Dec. 31	Depreciation	J	2 250
					Balance	c/d	22 750
			£25 000				£25 000
Jan. 1	Balance	b/d	22 750				

Depreciation

19..			£	19..			£
Dec. 31	Electric Generator Plant	J	2 250	Dec. 31	Profit and Loss A/c	T	2 250

Journal

		Dr.	Cr.
19..		£	£
Dec. 31	Depreciation	2 250	
	To Electric Generator Plant		2 250
	Depreciation at equal annual instalments		

5 'Depreciation' expresses the declining value of an asset immediately after its purchase owing to wear and tear.

Machinery

19.1			£	19.1				£
Jan. 1	Cash	CB	600	Dec. 31	Depreciation	J		225
					Balance	c/d		375
			£600					£600
19.2				19.2				
Jan. 1	Balance	b/d	375	Dec. 31	Depreciation	J		225
					Balance	c/d		150
			£375					£375
19.3								
Jan. 1	Balance	b/d	150					

6

Loose Tools

19..			£	19..			£
Jan. 1	Balance		1 425	Dec. 31	Transferred to		
					Trading A/c	T	1 425
Dec. 31	Transferred to						
	Trading A/c	J	1 623				

Trading Account
(Extract)

19..			£	19..			£
Dec. 31	Loose Tools,			Dec. 31	Loose Tools,		
	1st January		1 425		31st December		1 623

Balance Sheet
(Extract from Assets side)

CLAIMS	£		ASSETS	£
			Loose Tools,	
			31st December	1 623

7 Similar to **6**.

8

	Dr.	Cr.
	£	£
Capital; K. Watts		2 000·00
Drawings	240·00	
Machinery	1 500·00	
Furniture and Fittings	125·00	
Stock, 1st July, 19.1	1 345·00	
Purchases and Sales	4 731·00	7 249·00
Returns Inwards and Outwards	126·00	9·00
Carriage Inwards (on Purchases)	97·00	
Carriage Outwards (on Sales)	2·00	
Salaries	499·00	
Fire Insurance	5·00	
Expenses	492·00	
Discounts Allowed and Received	77·45	118·00
G. Leach	87·00	
F. Appleton		35·00
C. Peace		32·00
Cash in hand	38·00	
Cash at Bank	78·55	
	£9 443·00	£9 443·00

Trading Account
Year ended 30th June, 19.2

	£	£		£	£
Opening Stock 1st July, 19.1		1 345·00	Sales	7 249·00	
Purchases	4 731·00		Less Returns Inwards	126·00	
Add Carriage Inwards	97·00				7 123·00
	4 828·00				
Less Returns Outwards	9·00				
		4 819·00			
		6 164·00			
Less Closing Stock, 30th June, 19.2		1 041·00			
Cost of Sales		5 123·00			
Gross Profit		2 000·00			
		£7 123·00			£7 123·00

Journal		*Dr.*	*Cr.*
19.2		£ 12·50	£
June 30	Profit and Loss Account		
	To Depreciation		12·50
	10% Depreciation on Furniture and Fittings		

Net Profit £1 030·05; Balance Sheet totals £2 857·05.

9 Trial Balance totals £21 716; Gross Profit £1 729; Net Loss £143; Balance Sheet totals £14 304.

10

Trading Account
for year ended 31st December, 19..

	£	£		£	£
Opening Stock 1st January		452	Sales *Less* Returns	2 587	
Purchases	1 675		Inwards	73	
Less Returns Outwards	35				2 514
		1 640			
		2 092			
Less Closing Stock		432			
		1 660			
Manufacturing Wages		381			
Cost of Sales		2 041			
Gross Profit		473			
		£2 514			£2 514

Net Profit £128; Balance Sheet totals £1 720.

11

Machinery

1971			£	1972			£
Jan. 1	Cash		8 000	Jan. 1	Cash		1 722
1972					Depreciation		200
Jan. 1	Cash		4 800		Profit and		
					Loss A/c		68
				Dec. 31	Balance	c/d	10 800
			£12 800				£12 800
1973				1973			
Jan. 1	Balance	b/d	10 800	Jan. 1	Cash		1 625
	Profit and				Depreciation		400
	Loss A/c		25	Dec. 31	Balance	c/d	8 800
			£10 825				£10 825
1974							
Jan. 1	Balance	b/d	8 800				

Provision for Depreciation
(Machinery)

1972				1971			
Jan. 1	Machinery		200	Dec. 31	Profit and		
Dec. 31	Balance	c/d	1 680		Loss A/c		800
				1972			
				Dec. 31	Profit and		
					Loss A/c		1 080
			£1 880				£1 880
1973				1973			
Jan. 1	Machinery		400	Jan. 1	Balance	b/d	1 680
Dec. 31	Balance	c/d	2 160	Dec. 31	Profit and		
					Loss A/c		880
			£2 560				£2 560
				1974			
				Jan. 1	Balance	b/d	2 160

Balance Sheet (Extract)
as at 31st December, 1973

Machinery	8 800	
Less Depreciation	2 160	
		6 640

12   Gross Profit £20 010; Net Profit £7 250; Balance Sheet totals £47 290.

13

Trial Balance of J. Cooper
31st March, 19 . .

	£	£
Capital		30 000·00
Drawings	3 600·00	
Freehold Property	12 000·00	
Furniture and Fittings	1 500·00	
Stock, 19th March	14 360·00	
Purchases and Sales	68 170·00	83 250·00
Returns Inwards and Outwards	1 840·00	2 520·00
Rent and Rates	5 260·00	
Carriage Outwards	1 640·00	
Carriage Inwards	1 450·00	
Salaries and Commission	4 780·00	
Discount Received		150·00
Bad Debts	1 418·90	
H. Nelson		2 180·00
C. Blake		1 520·00
F. Drake	1 290·00	
G. Cook	940·00	
Cash in hand	490·00	
Cash at Bank	881·10	
	£119 620·00	£119 620·00

Gross Profit £10 700·00; Net Loss £2 398·90; Balance Sheet totals £27 701·10.

14   Gross Profit £6 890; Net Profit £4 461·25; Balance Sheet totals £13 621·25.
(Note to **14**: These figures are for six months only.)

15 *Note:* The provision for doubtful debts has been rounded up to the nearest pound.

Trading Profit and Loss Account
for year ended 31st December, 19 . .

	£	£		£	£
Opening Stock 1st Jan.		12 200	Sales	25 650	
Purchases	21 280		*Less* Returns	570	
Less Returns	140				25 080
		21 140			
		33 340			
Less Closing Stock					
31st December		13 800			
Cost of Sales		19 540			
Gross Profit c/d		5 540			
		£25 080			£25 080
Wages		3 120	Gross Profit b/d		5 540
Heating and Lighting		670	Discounts Received		130
Discounts Allowed		260			
Bad Debts		430			
Provision for Doubtful					
Debts (Nearest pound)		60			
Depreciation:					
Machinery	80				
Fixtures and Fittings	150				
Motor Van	180				
		410			
Net Profit to Capital		720			
		£5 670			£5 670

(*Note:* continued on KEY page 90).

Balance Sheet
as at 31st December 19..

	£	£		£	£	£
Capital	18 440		*Fixed Assets:*			
Add Net Profit	720		Machinery	800		
			Less Depreciation	80		
	19 160				720	
Less Drawings	240		Fixtures and Fittings	3 000		
		18 920	*Less* Depreciation	150		
					2 850	
			Motor Lorry	1 800		
			Less Depreciation	180		
					1 620	
						5 190
			Current Assets:			
			Stock 31st December		13 800	
			Debtors	2 420		
			Less Provision for			
			Bad Debts	60		
					2 360	
			Cash at Bank		3 470	
			Cash in hand		130	
					19 760	
			Current Liabilities:			
			Creditors		6 030	
			Working Capital			13 730
		£18 920				£18 920

16 The following introduces to the student the 'vertical' lay-out of the Final Accounts and the Balance Sheet. It is an alternative to the conventional two-sided method.

Trading and Profit and Loss Account

for year ended 31st December, 19 . .

	£	£	£
Sales	29 050·00		
Less Returns Inwards	670·00		
			28 380·00
Cost of Goods Sold:			
Stock, 1st January		12 300·00	
Purchases	24 280·00		
Less Returns Outwards	240·00		
		24 040·00	
		36 340·00	
Less Stock, 31st December		13 000·00	
Cost of Goods Sold			23 340·00
Gross Profit			5 040·00
Less Expenditure:			
Wages		3 020·00	
Rent and Rates		880·00	
Depreciation:			
Shop Fixtures	170·00		
Motor Vans	420·00		
		590·00	
Bad Debts		530·00	
Provision for Bad Debts		65·50	
		5 085·50	
Discounts Received	230·00		
Less Discounts Allowed	60·00		
		170·00	
			4 915·50
Net Profit			£124·50

(*Note:* Continued on KEY page 92).

Balance Sheet

as at 31st December, 19 . .

	£	Cost £	Depreci-ation £	Net £
Fixed Assets:				
Shop Fixtures		3 400·00	170·00	3 230·00
Motor Vans		2 800·00	420·00	2 380·00
		£6 200·00	£590·00	5 610·00
Current Assets:				
Stock, 31st December		13 000·00		
Debtors	2 620·00			
Less Provision for Bad Debts	65·50			
		2 554·50		
Cash at Bank		3 500·00		
Cash in hand		200·00		
			19 254·50	
Current Liabilities:				
Trade Creditors			6 630·00	
Working Capital				12 624·50
Net Value of Assets				£18 234·50
Represented by:				
Capital: M. Robinson				
Balance, 1st January			18 590·00	
Add Net Profit			124·50	
			18 714·50	
Less Drawings			480·00	
				18 234·50
Capital Employed and Owner's Equity				£18 234·50

17   Gross Profit £4 111; Net Loss £695·40; Balance Sheet totals £25 683·60.

18

Trading and Profit and Loss Account
for year ended 31st December, 1972

	£	£		£	£
Stock, 1st January		8 300	Sales		78 880
Purchases	63 420				
Less Drawings	52				
		63 368			
		71 668			
Less Stock, 31st Dec		9 420			
Cost of Sales		62 248			
Gross Profit c/d		16 632			
		£78 880			£78 880
Wages and Salaries	7 155		Gross Profit		16 632
Add amount due	247		Rent Receivable	735	
		7 402	*Add* Rent due	85	
Insurance and Rates	850			—	820
Less Prepayment	105				
	—	745			
Provision for Bad Debts		70			
General Expenses		2 165			
Bad Debts		465			
Net Profit T		6 605			
		£17 452			£17 452

Balance Sheet
as at 31st December, 1972

	£	£	£		£	£	£
Capital		22 000		*Fixed Assets*			
Add Net Profit		6 605		Freehold Property		11 000	
		28 605		Furniture		1 200	
							12 200
Less Drawings	2 570			*Current Assets*			
Purchases	52			Stock		9 420	
		2 622		Debtors	8 125		
			25 983	*Less* Provision for bad			
				debts	245		
						7 880	
				Rent Receivable due		85	
				Prepayments		105	
				Cash at bank		1 966	
						19 456	
				Current Liabilities			
				Creditors	5 426		
				Wages due	247		
						5 673	
				Working Capital			13 783
		£25 983					£25 983

Chapter 23   *Exercises*

1

	Trial Balance 30th Sept., 19..		Trial Balance 31st Dec., 19..	
	£	£	£	£
Capital		14 565·00		15 925·13
Drawings			100·00	
Premises	1 500·00		5 000·00	
Stock	8 320·00		5 125·00	
Purchases	1 750·00			
Sales		6 495·00		2 205·00
Wages	123·00		75·00	
Discounts Allowed	66·87			
The Pulman Sawmills Ltd.	3 575·00		3 575·00	
Wood and Lumber Co.	2 500·00		2 500·00	
Export Co.				2 205·00
Torquay Machinery Co.		3 013·00		
Cash in hand	35·00		160·00	
Cash at Bank	6 203·13			
Bank Overdraft				609·87
	£24 073·00	£24 073·00	£18 740·00	£18 740·00
Gross Profit		1 550·00		566·00
Net Profit		1 360·13		491·00
Balance Sheet totals		18 938·13		16 926·00

Capital Account

19..			£	19.. Jan. 1	Balance	b/d	£ 30 000

Current Account

19.. Jan./ Dec. Dec. 31	Cash: Drawings Balance	CB c/d	£ 364 220	19.. Dec. 31	Net Profit	T	£ 584
			£584				£584
				Jan. 1	Balance	b/d	220

2   Gross Profit £15 020; Net Profit £5 840; Balance Sheet totals £36 480.

> *Note on* **2**.
> '*Fixed*' *Capital*
> The owner's transactions with the firm, *e.g.* Drawings, are not shown in the Capital Account. They appear in a Current Account (as in Partnerships). In the present instance, G. Britton's Capital and Current Accounts would appear as in **1** above.

3 Refer to the following pages in the textbook:
      (i) Sales Day Book, pp. 66, 67.
      (ii) Cash Book, pp. 53, 54.
      (iii) Returns Outwards Book, p. 71.

4

S. Fane

19..			£	19..			£
Feb. 1	Balance	b/d	20·00	Feb. 17	Returns		
12	Sales	SDB	126·00		Inwards	RIB	14·00
20	,,	SDB	49·00	25	Cash Book	CB	150·00
				28	Balance	c/d	31·00
			£195·00				£195·00
Mar. 1	Balance	b/d	31·00	Mar. 1	Cash	CB	15·50
				31	Bad Debts	J	15·50
			£31·00				£31·00

5 Refer to the following pages in the textbook:
      (*a*) 117; (*b*) 117; (*c*) 118; (*d*) 117; (*e*) 118; (*f*) 118.

6 Refer to pp. 210–11 in the textbook.
Stock is valued either at cost price or current market value, whichever is the lower.

7   Wrong gross profit = £3 000

		−	+
		£	£
(*a*)	(i)		20
	(ii)	60	
	(iii)		649
	(iv)	9	
(*b*) Increase in gross profits		600	600
		£669	£669 £3 600 = Correct gross profit

(*c*) $\dfrac{GP}{Turnover} \times 100$, *i.e.* (i) $\frac{3000}{6000} \times 100 = 50\%$; (ii) $\frac{3000}{6000} \times 100 = 60\%$.

The higher gross profit represents a 10% increase.

8

Balance Sheet
as at 29th February, 19 . .

(i) Total Fixed Assets, £5 000.
(ii) Total Current Assets, £5 970.
(iii) Working Capital, £4 000.
(iv) Decrease Net Profit and therefore Decrease Capital; Decrease Fixed Assets by £1 000. (Assume Goodwill written off against profits.)
(v) Decrease Net Profit and therefore Capital by £200; Increase Current Liabilities by £200.
(vi) Increase Creditors by £300; Decrease Profit and therefore Capital by £300.
(vii) Williams is solvent; he possesses liquid assets of £4 000. Even if Roberts' loan were due and paid in the near future, Williams would still have £1 000 in liquid assets, plus the probable profit he would make on sale of stock.
(viii) Increase Debtors by £25; Increase Profit and therefore Capital by £25.

Balance Sheet
as at 29th February, 19 . . (Revised)

CLAIMS	£	£	ASSETS	£	£	£	£
Capital	5 100		*Fixed Assets*				
Less Net Loss	575		Freehold Premises				4 000
		4 525	*Current Assets*				
Long-Term Liabilities			Stock, 29th February		2 800		
Loan Account:			Debtors	1 500			
S. Roberts		3 000	*Less* Provision for Bad				
			Debts	75			
					1 425		
			Cash at Bank		1 700		
			Cash in hand		70		
						5 995	
			Current Liabilities				
			Creditors		2 270		
			Salaries due		200		
						2 470	
			Working Capital				3 525
		£7 525					£7 525

	− £	+ £
*Net Profit (given in original Balance Sheet)		900
(iv) Goodwill	1 000	
(v) Salaries due	200	
(vi) Purchases	300	
(vii) Provision for Bad Debts		25
Balance—Net Loss		575
	£1 500	£1 500

9

Balance Sheet
as at 31st December, 19 . .

CLAIMS	£	£	ASSETS	£	£	£	£
Capital			*Fixed Assets*				
Balance	8 000		Machinery at cost		7 000		
Add Net Profit	3 450		*Less* Accumulated				
			Depreciation		2 500		
	11 450					4 500	
Less Drawings	3 000		Furniture and Fittings			250	
		8 450					4 750
Loan Capital			*Current Assets*				
Loan Account			Stock		4 750		
(5 years)		1 000	Debtors	3 800			
			Less Provisions for Bad				
			Debts	182			
					3 618		
						8 368	
			Current Liabilities				
			Creditors:				
			Trade	3 240			
			Expenses	88			
					3 328		
			Bank Overdraft	340			
					3 668		
			Working Capital				4 700
Capital Employed		£9 450	Net Book Value of Assets				£9 450

10

		£			£
(*a*)	(i) Bank	1 190	(*b*) Gross Profit		1 100
	(ii) Stock	2 010	Net Profit		660
	(iii) Debtors	1 930	Fixed Assets		1 210
	(iv) Creditors:		Current Assets		5 130
	Trade	2 660	Current Liabilities		2 680
	Expenses	20	Working Capital		2 450
			Balance Sheet totals		3 660

Chapter 24   Exercises

1

J. Chanrai and Sons

19 . .		£	19 . .		£
Sept. 12	Bills Payable	500	Sept. 1	Purchases	500

Purchases

| 19 . .
Sept. 1 | J. Chanrai and
Sons | | £
500 | 19 . . | | | £ |

Bills Payable

| 19 . .
Dec. 5 | Cash | | £
500 | 19 . .
Sept. 12 | J. Chanrai and
Sons | | £
500 |

Cash Book (Extract)

| 19 . . | | | £ | 19 . .
Dec. 5 | Bills Payable | | £
500 |

2 and 3 Similar to **1.**

4 See example, p. 224 of textbook.

5

Trading and Profit and Loss Account
for year ended 30th June, 19 . .

		£			£
Stock, 1st July		2 106	Sales		10 527
Purchases		6 481			
		8 587			
Less Stock, 30th June		1 968			
		6 619			
Warehouse Salaries and Expenses		1 462			
Cost of Sales		8 081			
Gross Profit	c/d	2 446			
		£10 527			£10 527
Office Salaries		1 255	Gross Profit	b/d	2 446
Office Expenses		236	Bank Deposit Interest		23
Net Profit to Capital		1 054	Discount Received		76
		£2 545			£2 545

Balance Sheet
as at 30th June, 19..

Claims	£	£	Assets	£	£
Capital	18 000		*Fixed Assets*		
Add Net Profit	1 054		Freehold Premises		14 876
		19 054			
Current Liabilities			*Current Assets*		
Bills Payable	500		Stock, 30th June	1 968	
Creditors	2 274		Debtors	3 786	
		2 774	Bank Deposit	1 000	
			Cash at Bank	198	
					6 952
		£21 828			£21 828

6 Gross Profit £15 670; Net Profit £5 649; Balance Sheet totals £43 049.

Chapter 25   Exercises

1

R. Sinclair

19..			£	19..			£
Sept. 1	Sales		350	Sept. 1	Bills Receivable		350

Sales

19..			£	19..			£
				Sept. 1	R. Sinclair		350

Bills Receivable

19..			£	19..			£
Sept. 1	R. Sinclair		350	Nov. 4	Cash		350

Cash Book

19..			£	19..			£
Nov. 4	Bills Receivable		350				

2 Similar to **1**.

3

T. Yorke

19..			£	19..		£
Mar. 1	Sales		500	Mar. 1	Bills Receivable	500

Sales

19..			£	19..		£
				Mar. 1	T. Yorke	500

Bills Receivable

19..			£	19..		£
Mar. 1	T. Yorke		500	Mar. 2	Cash	500

Discount on Bills

19..			£	19..		£
Mar. 2	Cash: T. Yorke		10			

Cash Book

19..			£	19..		£
Mar. 2	Bills Receivable		500	Mar. 2	Discount on Bills (T. Yorke)	10

4 Similar to **3.**

5

L. T. Smith

19..			£	19..		£
Mar. 1	Sales		600	Mar. 1	Bills Receivable	600
June 1	Cash (Bill Dishonoured)		600			

Sales

19..			£	19..		£
				Mar. 1	L. T. Smith	600

Bills Receivable

19..			£	19..		£
Mar. 1	L. T. Smith		600	Mar. 4	Cash	600

Discount on Bills

19 . .		£	19 . .		£
Mar. 4	Cash: L. T. Smith	12			

Cash Book

19 . .		£	19 . .		£
Mar. 4	Bills Receivable	600	Mar. 4	Discount on Bills (L. T. Smith)	12
			June 1	L. T. Smith: Bill Dis- honoured	600

6 Similar to **5**.

7

Hull Ltd

19 . .		£	19 . .		£
Jan. 1	Balance	250	Jan. 16	Bills Receivable	250

Exeter and Co.

19 . .		£	19 . .		£
Jan. 1	Balance	400	Jan. 9	Bills Receivable	400

Bristol and Sons Ltd

19 . .		£	19 . .		£
Jan. 2	Bills Payable	300	Jan. 1	Balance	300

Cardiff Bros.

19 . .		£	19 . .		£
Jan. 23	Bills Payable	100	Jan. 1	Balance	100

Bills Receivable

19.. Jan. 9 16	Exeter and Co. Hull Ltd	£ 400 250	19.. Feb. 9	Cash: Bill Discounted Cash	£ 400 250
		£650			£650

Bills Payable

19.. Feb. 5	Cash	£ 300	19.. Jan. 2 23	Bristol and Sons Cardiff Bros.	£ 300 100

Discount on Bills

19.. Feb. 9	Cash: Exeter and Co.	£ 2	19..		£

Cash Book

19.. Feb. 9 Mar. 16	Bills Receivable Bills Receivable	£ 400 250	19.. Feb. 2 9	Bills Payable Discount on Bills	£ 300 2

8

Trial Balance
30th June, 19..

	£		£
Cash at Bank	3 185	Capital	9 700
Cash in hand	610	Sales	6 620
Drawings	300	Discounts Received	20
Purchases	540	Returns Outwards	70
Allowances	60	B. Luckworth	260
Bad Debts	370	R. Austin	580
Discounting Charges	5		
Wages	1 020		
Rent	150		
Stationery	150		
Stock, 1st June	7 000		
Plant and Machinery	1 430		
Furniture	210		
S. Jameson	2 220		
	£17 250		£17 250

Gross Loss £680; Net Loss £2 455; Balance Sheet totals £7 965.

N.B.: Adjustment No. 4: Interest on Capital £3; Debit Profit and Loss (Appropriation) Account; Credit Capital Account.

9

Trial Balance
31st July, 19..

	£		£
Cash in hand	50	Capital	15 000
Cash at Bank	1 162	Sales	2 810
Discounts Allowed	30	H. Hall	750
Purchases	750	M. Marks	1 370
Stock	7 850		
Tax and Insurance	400		
Salaries	250		
Expenses	50		
Rent	60		
Discount on Bills	18		
B. Bowen	1 160		
C. Charles	800		
Fixtures and Fittings	1 800		
Motor Van	5 400		
Drawings	150		
	£19 930		£19 930

Gross Profit £2 310; Net Profit £1 322·50; Balance Sheet totals £18 292·50.

10

Trial Balance
30th June, 19..

		Dr.	Cr.
		£	£
Capital: B. Somers			25 000
Drawings		2 750	
Furniture		6 000	
Stock, 1st June		33 450	
Purchases and Sales		102 000	114 000
Bills Payable			12 000
Bad Debts		360	
Discounts Allowed and Received		30	170
Discounting Charges		30	
Expenses		2 540	
Cash at Bank		4 010	
		£151 170	£151 170

Gross Profit £17 670; Net Profit £13 780; Balance Sheet totals £48 030.

Note:

B. Judge's Account

19..		£	19..		£
May 1	Balance	360	May 31	Cash	360
June 6	Cash: Cheque Dishonoured	360	June 17	Bad Debts	360

Chapter 26   *Exercises*

1

Goods Consigned Outwards

19.. Dec. 31 (end of year)	Trading A/c	T	£ 4 270	19.. April 1	Consignment Account	J	£ 4 270

Consignment to A. Dennis and Co., Kingston

19.. April 1			£	19.. Aug. 1			£
	Goods Consigned	J	4 270		A. Dennis and Co.	J	6 480
	Cash:						
	Freight	CB	20				
	Insurance	CB	720				
	A. Dennis and Co.:						
	Landing Charges	J	362				
	Commission	J	328				
	Profit and Loss						
	Account	T	780				
			£6 480				£6 480

A. Dennis and Co., Kingston

19.. Aug. 1			£	19.. Aug. 1			£
	Consignment Account: Gross Proceeds	J	6 480		Cash	CB	5 790
					Landing Charges	J	362
					Commission	J	328
			£6 480				£6 480

2

Goods Consigned Outwards

19.. Jan. 26	Trading A/c	T	£ 12 000	19.. Nov. 1	Consignment Account	J	£ 12 000

Consignment to Alva and Co., Buenos Aires

19..			£	19..			£
Nov. 1	Goods Consigned	J	12 000	Jan. 26	Alva and Co.		18 600
	Cash:						
	Packing	CB	45				
	Shipping and						
	Freight	CB	125				
	Insurance	CB	100				
Jan. 26	Alva and Co.:						
	Customs Duty	J	158				
	Landing Charges	J	40				
	Insurance	J	80				
	Warehousing	J	61				
	Commission	J	930				
	Profit and Loss						
	Account	T	5 061				
			£18 600				£18 600

Alva and Co., Buenos Aires

19..			£	19..			£
Jan. 26	Consignment			Jan. 26	Consignment		
	Account	J	18 600		Account:		
					Customs Duty	J	158
					Landing Charges	J	40
					Insurance	J	80
					Warehousing	J	61
					Commission	J	930
					Cash	CB	17 331
			£18 600				£18 600

3

Account Sales of Goods sold by New Way Co., Mombasa
for the account of Watson and Co., London

19..			£	£
	Part consignment sold for			1 210·00
	Deduct: Expenses		98·00	
	Commission		48·40	
				146·40
	Sight draft enclosed			£1 063·60

Goods Consigned Outwards

19..			£	19..			£
	Trading A/c	T	1 240·00		Consignment		
					Account	J	1 240·00

Consignment to New Way Co., Mombasa

19..			£		19..			£
	Goods Consigned	J	1 240·00			New Way Co.		
	Cash:					(Gross proceeds of		
	Freight	CB	83·00			part consignment		
	Insurance	CB	21·00			sold)	J	1 210·00
	New Way Co.					Stock of unsold		
	Sundry Charges	J	98·00			goods, including a		
	Commission	J	48·40			proportion of the		
	Profit and Loss					expenses	c/d	573·00
	Account	T	292·60					
			£1 783·00					£1 783·00
	Stock of unsold							
	goods	b/d	573·00					

New Way Co., Mombasa

19..			£		19..			£
	Consignment					Consignment		
	Account	J	1 210·00			Account:		
						Sundry Charges	J	98·00
						Commission	J	48·40
						Cash	CB	1 063·60
			£1 210·00					£1 210·00

4 Similar to **3.**
Net Profit £22.

		£
Unsold Stock		90
Add Proportion of charges		23
Total value of unsold stock	c/d	£113

Cash received from A. Trader £333.

5 Similar to **3** and **4.**
Net Profit £250.

		£
Unsold Stock		3 750
Add Proportion of charges		750
Total value of unsold stock		£4 500

Draft received £3 900.

6

A. Abdullahi, Karachi

19..		£	19..		£
April 1	Cash:		April 14	Cash:	
	Dock charges	50·00		Proceeds of	
	Carriage	100·00		Consignment	5 500·00
	Duty	200·00			
	Commission				
	2½%	137·50			
16	Cash	5 012·50			
		£5 500·00			£5 500·00

Chapter 27   Exercises

1

Statement of Profit
for year ended 31st March, 19.1

	£	£
Capital 31st March, 19..		61 920
Capital 31st March, 19.1		59 330
Net Decrease of Capital		2 590
Add Drawings	12 000	
,, Value of Goods taken out of Stock for own use	250	
		12 250
Net Profit		£9 660

2

P. Morgan's Statement of Affairs
as at 31st December, 19..

CLAIMS	£	ASSETS	£	£
Capital (excess of Assets over		*Fixed Assets*		
Liabilities)	30 750	Freehold Premises	10 000	
Current Liabilities		Plant and Machinery	6 000	
Creditors	18 750			16 000
		Current Assets		
		Stock	13 000	
		Debtors	17 500	
		Cash at Bank	3 000	
				33 500
	£49 500			£49 500

Statement of Profit
for year ended 31st December, 19..

		£
Capital, 1st January, 19..		55 000
Capital, 31st December, 19..		30 750
Net Decrease of Capital	(−)	24 250
Add Drawings	(+)	5 000
	(−)	19 250
Deduct the Value of Motor Car		
Paid into the Business	(−)	2 000
Net Loss for the year	(−)	£21 250

Alternatively:

	£
Capital, 31st December, 19..	30 750
Add Drawings	5 000
	35 750
Deduct Value of Motor Car	2 000
	33 750
Less Capital, 1st January, 19..	55 000
Net Loss for the year	£21 250

3

Trading and Profit and Loss Account
for year ended 31st December, 19..

		£			£	£
Stock, 1st January		8 760	Sales:			
Purchases		40 490	Credit		42 120	
			Cash		18 630	
		49 250				60 750
Less Stock, 31st December		8 540				
Cost of Sales		40 710				
Gross Profit	c/d	20 040				
		£60 750				£60 750
Wages		7 430	Gross Profit	b/d		20 040
General Expenses		6 270				
Provision for Bad Debts		1 500				
Depreciation:						
Machinery and Plant		580				
Net Profit to Capital		4 260				
		£20 040				£20 040

Balance Sheet of Samuel Wood
as at 31st December, 19..

CLAIMS	£	£	£	ASSETS	£	£	£
Capital, 1st January		31 500		*Fixed Assets*			
Add Amount paid in	2 000			Fixtures and			
„ Net Profit	4 260			Fittings			15 600
		6 260		Machinery and			
				Plant		4 200	
		37 760		*Add* Machinery			
Less Drawings	5 360			bought during the			
„ Goods	380			year		1 600	
		5 740				5 800	
			32 020	*Less* Depreciation		580	
							5 220
Current Liabilities							20 820
Creditors			8 160	*Current Assets*			
				Stock, 31st Dec.		8 540	
				Debtors	9 180		
				Less Drawings	380		
					8 800		
				Less Provision for			
				Bad Debts	1 500		
						7 300	
				Cash		3 520	
							19 360
			£40 180				£40 180

Calculations
Creditors' Control Account

19..			£	19..			£
Jan./				Jan. 1	Balance	b/d	7 210
Dec.	Cash		39 540	Dec. 31	*Purchases*		
Dec. 31	Balance	c/d	8 160		(Balance)		40 490
			£47 700				£47 700

Debtors' Control Account

19..			£	19..			£
Jan. 1	Balance	b/d	9 820	Jan./			
Dec. 31	*Sales*			Dec.	Cash		42 760
	(Balance)		42 120	Dec. 31	Balance	c/d	9 180
			£51 940				£51 940

4

Calculations
Creditors' Control Account

19..			£	19..			£
Jan./				Jan. 1	Balance	b/d	1 372
Dec.	Cash		6 490	Dec. 31	*Purchases*		6 706
Dec. 31	Balance	c/d	1 588				
			£8 078				£8 078

Debtors' Control Account

19..			£	19..			£
Jan. 1	Balance	b/d	2 218	Jan./			
Dec. 31	*Sales*		10 072	Dec.	Cash		9 805
					Bad Debts		115
				Dec. 31	Balance	c/d	2 370
			£12 290				£12 290

General Expenses

19..			£	19..			£
Jan./				Jan. 1	Balance	b/d	100
Dec.	Cash		2 515	Dec. 31	*Expenses*		2 676
Dec. 31	Petty Cash	T	140				
31	Balance	c/d	121				
			£2 776				£2 776

Petty Cash

19..			£	19..			£
Jan. 1	Balance		30	Dec. 31	Purchases		120
Dec. 31	Sales		250	31	*Expenses*	T	140
				31	Balance	c/d	20
			£280				£280

Receipts and Payments

19..			£	19..			£
Jan. 1	Balance		975	Dec. 31	Purchases		6 490
Dec. 31	Cash Sales		2 029		Expenses		2 515
	Debtors		9 805		Drawings		1 400
	Interest from				Income Tax		370
	Private				Balance	c/d	2 139
	Investments						
	paid into						
	Capital		105				
			£12 914				£12 914
Jan. 1	Balance	b/d	2 139				

Trading and Profit and Loss Account
for year ended 31st December, 19..

		£	£			£	£
Stock, 1st January			2 740	Sales:			
Purchases:				Credit		10 072	
Credit		6 706		Cash		2 029	
Petty Cash		120		Petty Cash		250	
			6 826				12 351
			9 566				
Less Stock, 31st Dec.			2 800				
			6 766				
Gross Profit	c/d		5 585				
			£12 351				£12 351
Expenses			2 676	Gross Profit	b/d		5 585
Bad Debts			115				
Depreciation:							
Fixtures and Fittings			35				
Net Trading Profit			2 759				
			£5 585				£5 585
Income Tax			370	Net Trading			
Net Profit to Capital			2 389	Profit	b/d		2 759
			£2 759				£2 759

Balance Sheet
as at 31st December, 19 . .

CLAIMS	£	£	ASSETS	£	£	£
Capital	15 776		*Fixed Assets*			
Additional Capital	105		Freehold Premises			11 000
Add Net Profit	2 389		Fixtures and Fittings		285	
	———		*Less* Depreciation		35	
	18 270				———	250
Less Drawings	1 400					———
	———	16 870				11 250
Current Liabilities			*Current Assets*			
Creditors:			Stock, 31st December		2 800	
Trade	1 588		Debtors	2 485		
Expenses	121		*Less* Bad Debts	115		
	———	1 709			2 370	
			Cash at Bank		2 139	
			Cash in hand		20	
					———	7 329
		———				———
		£18 579				£18 579

5(a)

Statement of Affairs
30th June, 19 . .

CLAIMS	£	ASSETS	£	£
Capital (excess of Assets over Liabilities)	26 540	*Fixed Assets*		
		Fixtures and Fittings	4 000	
		Motor Vans	3 700	
			———	7 700
Current Liabilities		*Current Assets*		
Creditors	10 740	Stock, 30th June	18 410	
		Debtors	4 700	
		Cash	6 470	
			———	29 580
	———			———
	£37 280			£37 280

Statement of Affairs
30th June, 19 . . (the following year)

CLAIMS	£	£	ASSETS	£	£	£
Capital (excess of Assets over Liabilities)		27 200	*Fixed Assets*			
			Fixtures and Fittings		3 600	
			Motor Van*		7 650	
					———	11 250
Current Liabilities			*Current Assets*			
Creditors	9 980		Stock, 30th June		17 620	
Heating and Lighting due	110		Debtors	3 500		
	———	10 090	*Less* Provision for Bad Debts	350		
					3 150	
			Rates Prepaid		290	
			Cash in hand and at Bank		4 980	
					———	26 040
		———				———
		£37 290				£37 290

Statement of Profit

	£
Capital, 1st July (previous year)	26 540
Capital, 30th June	27 200
Net increase of Capital	660
Add Drawings	12 000
Net Profit for the year	£12 660*

*The new motor van, in excess of the value of the old one, does not constitute *additional* capital. It was bought out of the existing resources of the business.

5(*b*) Fairfax's working capital, at the end of the second year, is the excess of Current Assets over Current Liabilities, *i.e.*

	£
Current Assets	26 040
Less Current Liabilities	10 090
Working Capital	£15 950

6(*a*)

Statement of Affairs
1st January, 19..

CLAIMS	£	£	ASSETS	£	£
Capital (excess of Assets over Liabilities)		1 463	*Fixed Assets*		
			Fixtures and Fittings	340	
			Motor Van	520	
					860
Current Liabilities			*Current Assets*		
Creditors:			Stock	1 368	
Trade	989		Debtors	428	
Expenses	17		Prepayments	23	
					1 819
	1 006				
Bank Overdraft	210				
		1 216			
		£2 679			£2 679

Statement of Affairs
31st December, 19. .

CLAIMS	£	£	ASSETS	£	£	£	£
Capital (excess of Assets over Liabilities)		1 467	*Fixed Assets*				
			Fixtures and Fittings		340		
Current Liabilities			*Less* Depreciation		17		
Creditors:					——	323	
Trade	1 037		Motor Van		520		
Expenses	14		*Less* Depreciation		104		
	—— 1 051				——	416	
						——	739
			Current Assets				
			Stock			1 294	
			Debtors		386		
			Less Bad Debts	38			
			,, Provision for Bad Debts	39			
				——	77		
					——	309	
			Prepayments			29	
			Cash			147	
						——	1 779
		——				——	——
		£2 518					£2 518

Statement of Profit

	£
Capital, 1st January	1 463
Capital, 31st December	1 467
Net Increase of Capital	4
Add Drawings	1 080
	1 084
Less Capital introduced	200
Net Profit	£884

6(b)

Trading Account
for year ended 31st December, 19. .

	£		£
Stock, 1st January	1 368	Sales	8 118
Purchases	6 310		
	7 678		
Less Stock, 31st December	1 294		
	6 384		
Gross Profit	1 734		
	£8 118		£8 118

Calculations

Debtors' Control Account

19 . .			£	19 . .			£
Jan. 1	Balance		428	Jan./			
Dec. 31	*Credit Sales*		8 118	Dec.	Cash		8 122
				Jan./			
				Dec.	Bad Debts		38
				Dec. 31	Balance	c/d	386
			£8 546				£8 546

Creditors' Control Account

19 . .			£	19 . .			£
Dec. 31	Cash		6 262	Jan. 1	Balance		989
31	Balance	c/d	1 037	Dec. 31	*Credit*		
					Purchases		6 310
			£7 299				£7 299

Chapter 28   Exercises

1

Income and Expenditure Account
for year ended 31st December, 19 . .

	£	£		£	£
Wages		1 040	Entrance Fees		60
Printing, Postage and			Subscriptions and		
and Stationery	280		Donations	2 100	
Add Amount due	40		*Add* Subscriptions	170	
		320	due		
Prizes		160			2 270
Expenses		120	Competition Fees		100
Rent		600	Profit on Refresh-		
Surplus to Accumu-			ments		420
lated Fund		610			
		£2 850			£2 850

Balance Sheet
as at 31st December, 19. .

CLAIMS	£	£	£	ASSETS	£
Accumulated Fund:				Equipment	870
Assets				Debtors	170
Cash	310			Cash	470
Equipment	550				
	——	860			
Add Surplus		610			
		——	1 470		
Creditors			40		
			————		————
			£1 510		£1 510

2

Income and Expenditure Account
for period ended 31st December, 19. .

	£	£		£	£
Wages		1 500	Entrance Fees		160
Printing and Postage	360		Subscriptions	2 200	
Add Amount due	20		*Add* Amount due	210	
		380			2 410
Stationery	30		Locker Rents	120	
Add Amount due	30		*Add* Amount due	20	
		60			140
Expenses		80	Interest on Deposit		20
Lighting and Fuel		190	Profit on Refresh-		
Tax and Insurance		540	ments		530
Surplus to Accumu-					
lated Fund		510			
		————			————
		£3 260			£3 260

Balance Sheet
as at 31st December, 19. .

CLAIMS	£	£	£	ASSETS	£	£
Accumulated Fund:				Clubhouse and		
Assets				Equipment	11 250	
Premises and Equip-				*Add* New Equipment	320	
ment	11 250					11 570
Bank Deposit	2 000			Debtors		230
Cash in hand	270			Bank Deposit		2 000
		13 520		Cash in hand		520
Add Surplus		510				
			14 030			
Subscriptions Prepaid			240			
Creditors			50			
			————			————
			£14 320			£14 320

3

Bar Trading Account
for year ended 31st December, 19 . .

	£		£
Stock, 1st January	210	Sales	1 840
Purchases	1 440		
	1 650		
Less Stock, 31st December	180		
	1 470		
Gross Profit to Income and Expenditure A/c	370		
	£1 840		£1 840

Income and Expenditure Account
for year ended 31st December, 19 . .

	£	£		£	£	£
Depreciation:			Gross Profit from Bar			370
Furniture		25	Trading Account			
Rent and Rates		645	Subscriptions received		845	
Wages		520	*Add* Subscriptions due		45	
Light and Heat	106				890	
Add Amount due	27					
		133	*Less* Subs included from			
Postage and			previous year	15		
Stationery		18	,, Bad Debt	5		
Insurance		7			20	
						870
			Dance and Social Receipts		347	
			Less Dance and Social			
			Expenses		269	
						78
			Furniture Account			6
			Net Loss to Accumulated			
			Fund			24
		£1 348				£1 348

Balance Sheet
as at 31st December, 19..

CLAIMS	£	£	ASSETS	£	£
Accumulated Fund, 1st January	781		*Fixed Assets*		
Less Net Loss	24		Furniture	481	
	——	757	*Less* Depreciation	25	
				——	456
Current Liabilities			*Current Assets*		
Creditors	175		Stock: Liquor 31st		
Light and Heat due	27		December	180	
	——	202	Debtors—Subs due	45	
			Insurance prepaid	4	
			Cash	274	
				——	503
		£959			£959

Journal			Dr.	Cr.
19..			£	£
Jan. 1	Furniture and Equipment		430	
	Stock: Liquor		210	
	Subscriptions due		20	
	Insurance prepaid		3	
	Cash		268	
	Creditors			150
	Capital			781
	Assets, Liabilities and Capital at this date		£931	£931

Calculations

Creditors' Control Account

19..				£	19..			£
Jan./					Jan. 1	Balance	b/d	150
Dec.	Cash			1 415	Dec. 31	*Purchases*		1 440
Dec. 31	Balance	c/d		175				
				£1 590				£1 590

Furniture

19..			£	19..			£
Jan. 1	Balance	b/d	430	Dec. 31	Cash (Sale of old furniture)		15
Dec. 31	Cash (New furniture)		60	31	Balance	c/d	481
31	Income and Expenditure Account (gain on sale of furniture)		6				
			£496				£496
Jan. 1	Balance	b/d	481				

Insurance

19..			£	19..			£
Jan. 1	Balance	b/d	3	Dec. 31	Balance	c/d	4
July 1	Cash		8	31	Income and Expenditure Account		7
			£11				£11
Jan. 1	Balance	b/d	4				

4

Income and Expenditure Account
for year ended 30th September, 19..

	£	£			£	£	£
Rent		200	Subscriptions			275	
Light and Heat	55		*Add* Subs due and				
Add Amount due	8		unpaid			25	
		63					300
Cleaning		26	Gross Proceeds				
Expenses		24	from Socials			500	
Surplus		302	*Less* Expenses			200	
							300
			Refreshments:				
			Sales			80	
			Opening Stock		15		
			Purchases		60		
					75		
			Less Closing Stock		10		
						65	
			Profit, refreshments				15
		£615					£615

Statement of Affairs
as at 30th September, 19 . .

CLAIMS	£	£		ASSETS	£	£
Accumulated Fund	258			Furniture and Fittings		190
Add Surplus	302			Stocks of Refreshments	10	
	——	560		Subscriptions due	25	
Light and Heat Account				Cash	343	
unpaid		8			——	378
		——				——
		£568				£568

5

Snack Bar Profit and Loss Account
for year ended 31st December, 1979

	£	£			£	£
Purchases: Cash	1 000			Sales		610
Less amount paid for 1978	266			Advertising	690	
	——			*Less* payments for 1978	128	
	734				——	
Add amount due for 1979	354				562	
	——					
	1 088			*Add* amount due 1979	107	
					——	669
Less closing stock	113					
(retained for special	——	975				
function in 1980)						
Stationery, etc.		144				
Profit: transferred to						
Income and Expenditure A/c		160				
		——				——
		£1 279				£1 279

Income and Expenditure Account
for year ended 31st December, 1979

	£	£			£	£
Rent		200		Subscriptions for 1979	1 257	
Salaries	875			*Add* subscriptions		
Add amount due	115			received in 1978	172	
	——	990			——	1 429
Stationery, etc.	265			Profit from Snack Bar		160
Less amount for Snack				Investment Income		200
Bar	144					
	——	121				
General Expenses		350				
Surplus for year		128				
		——				——
		£1 789				£1 789

Balance Sheet
as at 31st December, 1979

	£	£		£	£
Capital: 1st January			*Fixed Assets*		
1979	3 971		Furniture	510	
Add Surplus 31st December	128		*Add* new furniture	125	
	——	4 099		——	635
Current Liabilities			*Investments*		3 290
Sundry Creditors:			*Current Assets*		
Snack Bar	354		Stock	113	
Subscriptions in advance	162		Debtors	107	
Salaries accrued	115		Bank	585	
	——	631		——	805
		£4 730			£4 730

Note: Capital: 1st January 1979	*Assets*	*Claims*
	£	£
Furniture	510	
Investments	3 290	
Advertising pre-paid	128	
Subscriptions due	21	
Cash:	460	
Creditors		266
Subscriptions in advance		172
Capital: Excess of assets over liabilities		3 971
	——	——
	£4 409	£4 409

Chapter 29   Exercises

1

Manufacturing and Trading Account
for year ended 31st December, 19..

	£	£			£
Stocks, 1st January:			Stocks, 31st December:		
Raw Materials		22 370	Raw Materials		30 720
Partly Manufactured			Partly Manufactured		
Goods		5 860	Goods		3 170
Purchases of Raw Materials	293 140		Cost of Manufactured		
Carriage on Raw Materials	2 760		Goods (Balance)	c/d	613 310
		295 900			
Manufacturing Wages		219 840			
Manufacturing Power		94 310			
Manufacturing Expenses		8 920			
		£647 200			£647 200
Stock of Finished Goods			Sales		1 031 270
1st January		53 410			
Cost of Manufactured					
Goods	b/d	613 310			
		666 720			
Less Stock of Finished					
Goods, 31st December		60 950			
		605 770			
Purchases of Finished					
Goods		8 730			
		614 500			
Gross Profit		416 770			
		£1 031 270			£1 031 270

2

(1)

	£
Opening Stock of Raw Materials	1 700
Purchases of Raw Materials	15 000
	16 700
Less Closing Stock of Raw Materials	2 000
Cost of Raw Materials used	14 700

(2)

Wages	22 500
Factory Power	1 200
Cost of Goods Manufactured	£38 400

(3)

$$\frac{\text{Gross Profit (as given) } 11\,100}{\text{Turnover (or Sales) } 50\,000} \times 100 = 22 \cdot 2\% = \text{percentage of gross profit on Sales}$$

This is a barely satisfactory percentage of gross profit when the many overheads in the Profit and Loss Account (which may reasonably be anticipated) are taken into account.

3.

Manufacturing, Trading and Profit and Loss Account
for year ended 31st May, 19 . .

	£	£			£
ening Stocks, 1st June Raw Materials and ork in Progress		52 820	Cost of Manufactured Goods c/d		410 000
chases of Raw Materials	249 700				
d Carriage Inwards	820				
		250 520			
		303 340			
s Closing Stocks, 31st ay, of Raw Materials d Work in Progress		49 420			
		253 920			
tory Wages		118 610			
tory Expenses		37 470			
t of Manufactured Goods		£410 000			£410 000
ening Stock of Finished oods, 1st June		35 650	Sales	519 660	
st of Manufactured oods		410 000	*Less* Returns	1 170	
					518 490
		445 650			
s Closing Stock of nished Goods, 1st May		41 160			
st of Sales		404 490			
ss *Profit* c/d		114 000			
		£518 490			£518 490
vellers' Salaries and ommission		34 610	Gross Profit b/d		114 000
riage on Sales		5 960			
ce and Administration penses		27 430			
Profit		46 000			
		£114 000			£114 000

4

Manufacturing Account
(Extract)

	£	£	£
(a) Turnover, i.e. Sales	£247 000		
(b) Stock of Raw Materials, 1st January		27 840	
Purchases of Raw Materials		98 760	
		126 600	
Less Stock of Raw Materials, 31st December		23 210	
Cost of Raw Materials used			103 390
Add Factory Wages		78 500	
,, Power		1 060	
,, Rent and Rates		8 400	
,, Heat and Light		340	
			88 300
(c) Cost of Goods manufactured during year			£191 690

(d) Percentage of Profit on Capital:

$$\frac{\text{Net Profit}}{\text{Capital}} \times 100 = \frac{18\,700 \times 100}{85\,000} = 22\%$$

(e) Turnover		247 000	
Less Stock, 1st January (at selling price)		32 870	
		214 130	
Add Stock, 31st December (at selling price)		29 450	
Selling Price of Goods manufactured during year			£243 580

5(a)   See pages 276–278.

5(b)

Manufacturing and Trading Account
for year ended 30th June, 19..

		£	£			£
Stocks, 1st January:				Cost of		
Raw Materials			3 421	Manufactured		
Work in Progress			1 180	Goods	c/d	64 063
Purchases		17 843				
Add Carriage Inwards		261				
			18 104			
			22 705			
Less Stocks, 30th June:						
Raw Materials		3 121				
Work in Progress		1 420				
			4 541			
			18 164			
Factory Wages			33 248			
Factory Overheads			4 360			
Depreciation:						
Factory			2 050			
Machinery			6 241			
Cost of Manufactured Goods			£64 063			£64 063
Stock of Finished Goods,				Sales		98 341
1st January			5 932			
Cost of Manufactured Goods	b/d		64 063			
			69 995			
Less Stock of Finished						
Goods, 30th June			6 360			
			63 635			
Warehouse Wages			7 120			
Warehouse Overheads			2 830			
Depreciation:						
Warehouse			870			
Warehouse Fittings			130			
Cost of Sales			74 585			
Gross Profit			23 756			
			£98 341			£98 341

6(*a*)

Manufacturing, Trading and Profit and Loss Account of C.D.
for year ended 31st December, 19. .

	£	£			£
Materials Consumed (*or used*)			Cost of Goods Produced to		
Stock, 1st January		4 000	Trading Account	c/d	82 000
Purchases	14 000				
Add Carriage	700				
		14 700			
		18 700			
Less Stock, 31st December		3 400			
Cost of Materials used		15 300			
Wages	48 000				
Add National Insurance	700				
		48 700			
Prime Cost		64 000			
Factory Overheads					
Workshop Expenses	2 100				
,, Insurance	900				
,, Power and Lighting	3 300				
Depreciation of Plant and Workshop Tools	10 000				
		16 300			
Direct Cost of Production		80 300			
Add Work in Progress, 1st January		4 500			
		84 800			
Less Work in Progress, 31st December		2 800			
Cost of Goods Produced		£82 000			£82 000
Cost of Finished Goods Sold			Sales of Finished Goods		113 000
Stock of Finished Goods, 1st January		3 000			
Cost of Goods Produced	b/d	82 000			
		85 000			
Less Stock of Finished Goods, 31st December		4 200			
Cost of Sales		80 800			
Gross Profit	c/d	32 200			
		£113 000			£113 000

	£	£			£
Administration			Gross Profit	b/d	32 200
Office Expenses, Salaries and Insurance	11 200				
Postages and Telephone	850				
		12 050			
Selling and Distribution					
Advertising	800				
Carriage on Sales	4 800				
		5 600			
Net Trading Profit	c/d	14 550			
		£32 200			£32 200
Interest on Capital		6 000	Net Trading Profit	b/d	14 550
C.D.'s Salary		5 000			
Net Profit Transferred to Capital Account		3 550			
		£14 550			£14 550

6(*b*)

The percentage of net trading profit on turnover is $\frac{14550}{113000} \times 100 = 12\cdot8\%$ (approx.); a fairly good profit, especially if the provision of £10 000 as depreciation on Plant and Workshop tools is taken into account.

The percentage of net trading profit on Capital is $\frac{14550}{120000} \times 100 = 12\cdot1\%$ (approx.). Of this percentage C.D. has appropriated $\frac{6000}{120000} \times 100 = 5\%$ (£6 000) as interest on his investment in the business (£120 000), and a further $\frac{5000}{120000} \times 100 = 4\cdot1\%$ (approx.) (£5 000) as salary to himself. This leaves $12\cdot1 - (5 + 4\cdot1) = 12\cdot1 - 9\cdot1 = 3\%$ net on his investment of £120 000 to be ploughed back into his business (*i.e.* added to Capital). A return of $12\cdot1\%$ on capital invested is a fairly good return.

Alternative method

Manufacturing, Trading and Profit and Loss Account of C.D.

for year ended 31st December, 19 . .

19 . .		£	£	£
Sales of Finished Goods				113 000
Materials Consumed (or used)				
Stock, 1st January			4 000	
Purchases		14 000		
Add Carriage		700		
			14 700	
			18 700	
Less Stock, 31st December			3 400	
Cost of Materials used			15 300	
Wages		48 000		
Add National Insurance		700		
			48 700	
Prime Cost			64 000	
Factory Overheads				
Workshop Expenses		2 100		
,, Insurance		900		
,, Power and Lighting		3 300		
Depreciation on Plant and				
Workshop Tools		10 000		
			16 300	
Direct Cost of Production			80 300	
Add Work in Progress, 1st January		4 500		
Less Work in Progress, 31st December		2 800		
			1 700	
Cost of Goods Produced			82 000	
Stock of Finished Goods,				
1st January			3 000	
			85 000	
Less Stock of Finished Goods,				
31st December			4 200	
Cost of Sales				80 800
Gross Profit				32 200
Administration				
Office Expenses, Salaries and				
Insurance		11 200		
Postages and Telephone		850		
			12 050	
Selling and Distribution				
Advertising		800		
Carriage on Sales		4 800		
			5 600	
				17 650
Net Trading Profit				14 550
Interest on Capital			6 000	
C.D.'s Salary			5 000	
				11 000
Net Profit Transferred to Capital				
Account				£3 550

Chapter 30 Exercises

1 to **3**   The answers to these questions are clearly stated in Chapter 30.

5

Funds Flow Statement of the Georgia Company for Year 19.1

	NATURE OF DIFFERENCE	AMOUNT OF DIFFERENCE	
		Uses £	Sources £
Capital	Increase in Claim		7 000
Retained Profits	Increase in Claim		4 000
Current Liabilities			
Creditors	Increase in Claim		5 500
Bank Overdraft	Decrease in Claim	3 500	
Fixed Assets			
Plant	Decrease in Asset		500
Vehicles	Increase in Asset	7 500	
Current Assets			
Stocks	Increase in Asset	9 000	
Debtors	Decrease in Asset		4 000
Bank	Increase in Asset	1 000	
		£21 000	£21 000

In practice this would be set out as follows:

SOURCE OF FUNDS

	£
Increase in Capital	7 000
Increase in Retained Profits	4 000
Increase in Creditors	5 500
Reduction in Debtors	4 000
Disposal of Plant	500
	£21 000

USE OF FUNDS

	£
Increase in Vehicles	7 500
Increase in Stockholding	9 000
Increase in Bank Balance	4 500
	£21 000

Funds Flow Statement of the Georgia Company for year 19.2

SOURCE OF FUNDS

	£
Change of Bank Balance to Overdraft	10 000
Reduction in Stockholding	3 500
Disposal of Plant	500
	£14 000

USE OF FUNDS

	£
Decrease in Retained Profits	2 000
Decrease in Creditors	5 000
Increase in Debtors	5 000
Increase in Vehicles	2 000
	£14 000

Note: In the above two Funds Flow Statements, changes in Fixed Assets are assumed to be the result of Disposals and Purchases.

4

Revised Funds Flow Statement of the Georgia Company for year 19.1

SOURCE OF FUNDS

	£	£
Increase in Capital		7 000
Increase in Retained Profits	4 000	
Add back: Drawings	5 000	
Depreciation	2 000	
Loss on sale of vehicle	300	
		11 300
Increase in Creditors		5 500
Disposal of Vehicle		200
Reduction in Debtors		4 000
		£28 000

USE OF FUNDS

	£
Drawings	5 000
Increase in Vehicles	9 500
Increase in Stockholding	9 000
Increase in Bank Balance	4 500
	£28 000

Revised Funds Flow Statement of the Georgia Company for year 19.2

SOURCE OF FUNDS

	£	£	£
Change of Bank Balance to Overdraft			10 000
Reduction in Retained Profits		2 000	
Less: Drawings	6 000		
Depreciation	3 500		
		9 500	
		7 500	
Less: Bad Debts Written off		1 000	
			6 500
Reduction in Stockholding			3 500
			£20 000

USE OF FUNDS

	£
Drawings	6 000
Decrease in Creditors	5 000
Increase in Debtors	4 000
Increase in Vehicles	5 000
	£20 000

Chapter 31   Exercises

1 to 9   The answers to all these questions are clearly stated in Chapter 31.

Chapter 32   Exercises

Note on the Exercises
The method used in the solutions of Exercises in Chapter 32 is an alternative to that shown in the textbook. But the textbook method is also shown in the solution of Question 1. Here we show simply the purchaser's journal opening entries. The Goodwill represents the excess of the purchase price paid to the vendor plus other liabilities, less the assets. Where assets or liabilities have been revalued on purchase, it is the new values which should be shown in the opening entries.

1

	Journal of R. B. Graham	*Dr.*	*Cr.*
19..		£	£
Jan. 1	Machinery	1 500	
	Fittings and Fixtures	160	
	Stock	2 180	
	Debtors	1 550	
	Goodwill (Excess of Liabilities over Assets)	522	
	Creditors		1 412
	Vendor: R. Foreman (Purchase price of business)		4 500
		£5 912	£5 912

Assets and Liabilities acquired from vendor on purchasing his business.

		Dr.	*Cr.*
19..		£	£
Jan. 1	R. Foreman: Vendor	4 500	
	Capital Account		4 500
	Purchase price of business paid by R. B. Graham transferred		

R. B. Graham's Balance Sheet
as at 1st January, 19..

CLAIMS	£	ASSETS	£	£
Capital		*Goodwill*		522
R. B. Graham	4 500	*Fixed Assets*		
		Machinery	1 500	
		Fittings and Fixtures	160	
				1 660
Current Liabilities		*Current Assets*		
Creditors	1 412	Stock	2 180	
		Debtors	1 550	
				3 730
	£5 912			£5 912

1 (Alternative method).

Journal of R. B. Graham		Dr.	Cr.
19..		£	£
Jan. 1	Business Purchase	4 500	
	Vendor: R. Foreman		4 500
	Purchase price as agreed		
Jan. 1	Machinery	1 500	
	Fittings and Fixtures	160	
	Stock	2 180	
	Debtors	1 550	
	Business Purchase Account		5 390
	Assets acquired	£5 390	£5 390
Jan. 1	Business Purchase Account	1 412	
	Creditors		1 412
	Liabilities taken over from vendor	£1 412	£1 412
Jan. 1	Vendor: R. Foreman	4 500	
	R. B. Graham: Capital		4 500
	Purchase price paid to vendor		
Jan. 1	Goodwill	522	
	Business Purchase Account		522
	Value of Goodwill acquired		

LEDGER
Business Purchase Account

19..			£	19..			£
Jan. 1	Vendor	J	4 500	Jan. 1	Sundry Assets acquired	J	5 390
	Creditors	J	1 412		Goodwill: Being balance		522
			£5 912				£5 912

2

Journal of R. Jacobs and B. Mosley		Dr.	Cr.
19..		£	£
Jan. 1	Premises	4 800	
	Machinery	2 750	
	Furniture and Fittings	100	
	Debtors	1 920	
	Stock	2 800	
	Goodwill	1 270	
	Creditors		2 640
	Vendor: B. Macintosh		11 000
		£13 640	£13 640

Assets and Liabilities acquired from vendor on purchasing his business.

Dr.				Cash Book			Cr.
19..			£	19..			£
Jan. 1	Capital A/cs:			Jan. 1	B. Macintosh:		
	R. Jacobs		6 000		Vendor		11 000
	B. Mosley		6 000				

LEDGER
Vendor: B. Macintosh

19..			£	19..			£
Jan. 1	Cash	CB	11 000	Jan. 1	Balance	J	11 000

Capital Accounts

19..		R. Jacobs £	B. Mosley £	19..		R. Jacobs £	B. Mosley £
				Jan. 1	Cash	6 000	6 000

Examination questions sometimes require candidates to show Journal entries *only* for every transaction. In such a situation the above cash ledger entries would appear in the Journal as follows:

Journal of R. Jacobs and B. Mosley		Dr.	Cr.
19..		£	£
Jan. 1	Cash	12 000	
	Capital: R. Jacobs		6 000
	B. Mosley		6 000
	Capital in cash contributed by	£12 000	£12 000
	R. Jacobs and B. Mosley		
1	Vendor: B. Macintosh	11 000	
	Cash		11 000
	Purchase price of business paid by cheque on firm's bank Balance Sheet totals £14 640.		

3

Journal of T. B. Jones and A. M. Wilmot

		Dr. £	Cr. £
19..			
Jan. 1	Freehold Premises	4 000	
	Machinery and Plant	1 800	
	Furniture and Fittings	200	
	Stock	2 750	
	Debtors	1 840	
	Goodwill	2 075	
	Creditors		2 165
	Vendor: J. B. Duncan		10 500
	Assets and Liabilities acquired from vendor on purchasing his business	£12 665	£12 665
1	Vendor: J. B. Duncan	10 500	
	Capital Accounts:		
	T. B. Jones		5 250
	A. M. Wilmot		5 250
	Purchase price of business paid by the partners in equal shares transferred	£10 500	£10 500
1	Cash	1 500	
	Capital Accounts:		
	T. B. Jones		750
	A. M. Wilmot		750
	Cash contributed to the capital of the firm by the partners	£1 500	£1 500

Examiners sometimes require Journal entries *only*

Balance Sheet
as at 1st January, 19..

CLAIMS	£	£	ASSETS	£	£
Capital Accounts			Goodwill		2 075
T. B. Jones	6 000		*Fixed Assets*		
A. M. Wilmot	6 000		Freehold		
	——	12 000	Premises	4 000	
			Machinery and Plant	1 800	
			Furniture and Fittings	200	
				——	6 000
Current Liabilities			*Current Assets*		
Creditors		2 165	Stock	2 750	
			Debtors	1 840	
			Cash at Bank	1 500	
				——	6 090
		£14 165			£14 165

4 Goodwill £3 150; Balance Sheet totals £33 400.

5

Balance Sheet of Barnett and Marsden
as at 1st January, 19. .

CLAIMS	£	£	ASSETS	£	£
Capital Accounts			*Goodwill*		1 000
Barnett	9 750		*Fixed Assets*		
Marsden	2 070		Premises	2 000	
	———	11 820	Furniture and Fittings	300	
				———	2 300
Current Liabilities			*Current Assets*		
Bills Payable	500		Stock	7 500	
Creditors	2 040		Debtors	2 400	
	———	2 540	Bills Receivable	200	
			Cash at Bank	960	
				———	11 060
		£14 360			£14 360

Marsden's Journal		Dr.	Cr.
19. .		£	£
Capital		930	
(*a*) Furniture and Fittings			180
(*b*) Debtors			150
(*c*) Stock			600
		£930	£930
(*a*) Furniture retained by Mr Marsden for own use			
(*b*) Bad debts written off			
(*c*) Reduction on re-valuation			

Barnett's Journal		Dr.	Cr.
19. .		£	£
Capital		250	
Stock			250
Reduction on re-valuation			
Goodwill		1 000	
Capital			1 000
Agreed value of Goodwill on amalgamation			

6

Balance Sheet of Lucas and Cave
as at 1st January, 19 . .

CLAIMS	£	£	ASSETS	£	£	£
Capital Accounts			*Goodwill*			10 000
Lucas	72 475		*Fixed Assets*			
Cave	2 274		Plant and Machinery		31 000	
		74 749	Fittings		4 140	
						35 140
Current Liabilities			*Current Assets*			
Creditors		9 200	Stock		19 359	
			Debtors	11 000		
			Less Provision for			
			Bad Debts	550		
					10 450	
			Cash at Bank		9 000	
						38 809
		£83 949				£83 949

7 Similar to **6**.
Goodwill £8 000; Balance Sheet totals £109 745.

Chapter 33   Exercises

1

Capital Accounts

			D. P. Graves £	E. Coffin £	19 . .			D. P. Graves £	E. Coffin £
.					Dec. 31	Balances	b/d	5 000	3 000

Current Accounts

19 . .			D. P. Graves £	E. Coffin £	19 . .			D. P. Graves £	E. Coffin £
Jan./ Dec.	Cash	CB	6 000	5 000	Dec. 31	Share of			
Dec. 31	Balances	c/d	6 500	2 500		Profit	T	12 500	7 500
			£12 500	£7 500				£12 500	£7 500
					Jan. 1	Balances	b/d	6 500	2 500

2 Capital and Current Accounts similar to **1.**

Balance Sheet

CLAIMS	£	£	£	ASSETS	£	£
Capital Accounts						
J. Groom		2 000				
T. B. Bride		1 000				
			3 000			
Current Accounts						
J. Groom:						
⅔ Share of Profit	5 200					
Less Drawings	4 000					
		1 200				
T. B. Bride:						
⅓ Share of Profit	2 600					
Less Drawings	3 000					
		[400]				
			800			

3 Similar to **1.**
Current Accounts, Credit Balances: Childs £1 300; Carr £2 500.

4

Capital Accounts

19 . .			G. Reader £	A. Storey £	19 . .			G. Reader £	A. Store £
Dec. 31	Balances	c/d	3 000	3 000	Jan. 1	Balances	b/d	2 500	2 50●
					July 1	Cash		500	50●
			£3 000	£3 000				£3 000	£3 0●
					Jan. 1	Balances	b/d	3 000	3 0●

Current Accounts

19 . .			G. Reader £	A. Storey £	19 . .			G. Reader £	A. Stor £
Jan./ Dec.	Cash	CB	3 200	3 200	Dec. 31	Share of Profit	T	5 600	2 8●
Dec. 31	Balance	c/d	2 400		31	Balance	c/d		4●
			£5 600	£3 200				£5 600	£3 2●
Jan. 1	Balance	b/d		400	Jan. 1	Balance	b/d	2 400	

5

Trading and Profit and Loss Account
for year ended 31st December, 19..

		£		£	£
Stock, 1st January		1 939	Sales and		
Purchases		4 307	Services:		
			Motor Cars	6 430	
		6 246	Petrol, Oils, etc.	2 948	
Less Stock			Repairs to Cars	989	
31st December		2 621			10 367
		3 625			
Wages		2 100			
Electric Power		427			
Gross Profit	c/d	4 215			
		£10 367			£10 367
Advertising		75	Gross Profit	b/d	4 215
Wages		412			
Electricity		48			
Expenses		156			
Insurance		89			
Net Trading Profit	c/d	3 435			
		£4 215			£4 215
Share of Profit:	T		Net Trading Profit	b/d	3 435
Palmer, ⅗		2 061			
Pye, ⅖		1 374			
		£3 435			£3 435

Balance Sheet
as at 31st December, 19..

	£	£		£	£
Capital Accounts:			*Fixed Assets:*		
Palmer	11 400		Freehold Property	1 500	
Pye	7 600		Plant and Machinery	750	
		19 000	Breakdown lorry	925	
					16 675
Current Accounts:			*Current Assets:*		
Palmer:			Stock, 31st December	2 621	
Balance (Cr.)	182		Debtors	1 413	
Share of Profit	2 061		Cash at Bank	508	
	2 243				4 542
Less Drawings	1 582				
		661			
Pye:					
Balance (Dr.)	230				
Drawings	912				
	1 142				
Share of Profit	1 374				
		232			
Current Liabilities:					
Creditors		1 324			
		£21 217			£21 217

Alternative (preferable) method

Balance Sheet
as at 31st December, 19..

Capital Accounts:				Fixed Assets:		
Palmer		11 400		Freehold Premises	15 000	
Pye		7 600		Plant and Machinery	750	
		———	19 000	Breakdown lorry	925	
					———	16 675
Current Accounts:	*Palmer*	*Pye*				
Balances	182	[230]		*Current Assets:*		
Share of Profits	2 061	1 374		Stock 31st		
	———	———		December	2 621	
	2 243	1 144		Debtors	1 413	
Drawings	1 582	912		Cash at Bank	508	
	———	———			———	
	661	232			4 542	
	═══	═══	893			
				Current Liabilities:		
				Creditors	1 324	
				Working Capital		3 218
			———			———
			£19 893			£19 893
			═══			═══

6

Trading and Profit and Loss Account
for year ended 31st March, 19 . .

		£	£			£	£
Stock, 1st April, 19.1			37 420·00	Sales			166 450·00
Purchases		50 430·00					
Carriage Inwards		1 680·00					
			52 110·00				
			89 530·00				
Less Stock, 31st March, 19.2			30 821·00				
			58 709·00				
Manufacturing Wages			39 000·00				
Manufacturing Expenses			8 700·00				
Gross Profit	c/d		60 041·00				
			£166 450·00				£166 450·00
				Gross Profit	b/d		60 041·00
Depreciation: Furniture and Fixtures		90·00		Discounts Received			820·00
Plant and Machinery		1 950·00					
			2 040·00				
Bad Debts			720·00				
Prov. for Doubtful Debts			150·00				
Discounts Allowed			3 870·00				
Rent and Rates			2 300·00				
Salaries			7 200·00				
Insurance			340·00				
Sundry Expenses			1 160·00				
Net Trading Profit	c/d		43 081·00				
			£60 861·00				£60 861·00
				Net Trading Profit	b/d		43 081·00
Share of Profit: Sinclair, $\frac{3}{5}$	T		25 848·60				
Clark, $\frac{2}{5}$			17 232·40				
			43 081·00				43 081·00

Trial Balance of D. Sinclair and B. Clark (*abridged*)

	£		£
Debit side total	275 090·00	Capital: Sinclair	68 830·00
		Creditors	38 140·00
		Provision for bad debts	850·00
		Discounts received	820·00
		Sales	166 450·00
	£275 090·00		£275 090·00

Balance Sheet
as at 31st March, 19.2

CLAIMS	£	£	£
Capital Accounts			
Sinclair	68 830·00		
*Clark (Dr.)	2 300·00		
			66 530·00
Current Accounts			
Sinclair:			
Share of Profit	25 848·60		
Less Drawings	18 000·00		
		7 848·60	
Clark:			
Share of Profit	17 232·40		
Less Drawings	12 000·00		
		5 232·40	
			13 081·00
Current Liabilities			
Creditors			38 140·00
			£117 751·00

ASSETS	£	£	£	£
Fixed Assets				
Plant and Machinery		26 000·00		
Less Depreciation		1 950·00		
			24 050·00	
Furniture and Fixtures		1 800·00		
Less Depreciation		90·00		
			1 710·00	
				25 760·00
Current Assets				
Stock, 31st March 19.2		51 900·00		
Debtors			30 821·00	
Less Bad Debts	720·00			
,, Provision for Bad Debts	1 000·00			
		1 720·00		
			50 180·00	
Cash at Bank		9 770·00		
Cash in hand		1 220·00		
			10 990·00	
				91 991·00
				£117 751·00

*Clark's Capital Account deficiency could be closed by the transfer of an appropriate amount from his Current Account.

7

Joint Venture with C. Nelson

19..		£	19..		£
	Cash: Nelson for purchase of Flour	4 800·00		Cash: proceeds of sale of Flour	12 500·00
	Cash: Expenses	56·00			
	Profit and Loss Account: ½ Share of Profit	1 172·50			
	Cash to C. Nelson	6 471·50			
		£12 500·00			£12 500·00

Joint Venture Account

19..		£	19..		£
	Purchase of Flour	9 600·00		Proceeds of Sales of Flour	12 500·00
	Unloading	185·00			
	Carriage	103·00			
	Warehousing	211·00			
	Expenses	56·00			
	Bennett: ½ Share of Profit	1 172·50			
	Nelson: ½ Share of Profit	1 172·50			
		£12 500·00			£12 500·00

8

Joint Venture Account

19..		£	19..		£
	Purchases	1 130		Proceeds of Sales	1 590
	Carriage	21			
	Insurance	9			
	Commission	10			
	Share of Profit:				
	A. Blake, ⅔ Share	280			
	M. Day, ⅓ Share	140			
		£1 590			£1 590

9

Joint Venture with Bell

19..		£	19..		£
June 25	Cash: Purchase of three pictures	1 600·00	July 17	Cash: Proceeds of Sale of one picture	600·00
	Expenses	25·00	Aug. 5	Cash: Bell	684·00
July 25	Carriage (Picture sent to Bell)	7·00	Sept. 30	Unsold picture at agreed valuation	400·00
	Commission	30·00	Oct. 5	Cash from Bell	83·25
	Profit and Loss Account: ½ Share of Profit	105·25			
		£1 767·25			£1 767·25

Joint Venture Account

19..		£	£	19..		£
June 25	Purchases		2 950·00	July 17	Proceeds of Sale of Pictures	600·00
	Expenses		35·00	Aug. 5	Proceeds of Sale of Pictures	720·00
July 25	Carriage		7·00		Proceeds of Sale of Pictures	850·00
	Commission		30·00		Proceeds of Sale of Pictures	780·00
	,,		36·00			
29	,,		81·50	Sept. 30	Picture taken over by Adams at agreed value	400·00
	Share of Profit:					
	Adams: ½ Share	105·25				
	Bell: ½ Share	105·25				
			210·50			
			£3 350·00			£3 350·00

10

In A's Ledger   ### Joint Venture with B

19..		£	19..		£
	Cash:			Cash from B	2 400·00
	Purchases	4 800·00		,, ,, ,,	3 355·87½
	Freight	160·00			
	Unloading	70·00			
	Carriage	93·00			
	Profit and Loss Account: ½ Share of Profit	632·87½			
		£5 755·87½			£5 755·87½

In B's Ledger — **Joint Venture with A**

19..		£	19..		£
	Cash:			Proceeds of Sale	6 500·00
	To A	2 400·00			
	Expenses	30·00			
	Discounting				
	Charges	81·25			
	Profit and Loss				
	Account: ½ Share				
	of Profit	632·87½			
	Cash to A	3 355·87½			
		£6 500·00			£6 500·00

Chapter 34   Exercises

1

Trading and Profit and Loss Account
for year ended 31st December, 19..

		£			£
Stock 1st January		2 529	Sales		40 025
Purchases		24 597			
		27 126			
Less Stock 31st December		2 876			
Cost of Sales		24 250			
Gross Profit	c/d	15 775			
		£40 025			£40 025
Rent and Rates		992	Gross Profit	b/d	15 775
Insurance		133			
Salaries		6 319			
General Expenses		1 197			
Lighting and Heating		218			
Depreciation:					
Motor Vans (1 year)		700			
Net Trading Profit	c/d	6 216			
		£15 775			£15 775
Share of Profit:			Net Trading Profit		6 216
Laxton		3 108			
Bexley		3 108			
		£6 216			£6 216

Balance Sheet
as at 31st December, 19..

	£	£		£	£
Capital Accounts			*Fixed Assets*		
Laxton	3 250		Motor Vans	3 500	
Bexley	3 250		*Less* Depreciation	1 400	
		6 500			2 100
Current Accounts			*Current Assets*		
Laxton	1 868		Stock	2 876	
Bexley	2 020		Debtors	3 349	
		3 888	Prepayment:		
Current Liabilities			Insurance		
Creditors: Trade	2 048		Cash at Bank	24	
Rates	56			4 143	
		2 104			10 392
		£12 492			£12 492

CALCULATIONS
Total Debtors

1970				1971			
Dec. 31	Balance		3 171	Dec. 31	Cash		39 847
31	Sales*		40 025	Dec. 31	Balance	c/d	3 349
			£43 196				£43 196

Total Creditors

1971				1970			
Dec. 31	Cash		24 171	Dec. 31	Balance		1 622
31	Balance	c/d	2 048	31	Purchases*		24 597
			£26 219				£26 219

Rent and Rates

1971				1970			
Dec. 31	Balance Rates	c/d	56	Dec. 31	Balance: Rates		44
31	Cash: Rent and		980	31	Rent and Rates		
	Rates				for 1971*		992
			£1 036				£1 036

Insurance

1970				1970			
Dec. 31	Balance		28	Dec. 31	Balance	c/d	24
31	Cash		129	31	Insurance for		
					1971*		133
			157				157

Current Accounts

			Laxton	Bexley				Laxton	Bexley
1970					1970				
Dec. 31	Drawings		1 382	1 296	Dec. 31	Share of			
31	Balance	c/d	522	608		Share of profit		1 904	1 904
			£1 904	£1 904				£1 904	£1 904
1971					1971				
Dec. 31	Drawings		1 762	1 696	Jan. 1	Balances	b/d	522	608
31	Balances	b/d	1 868	2 020	Dec. 31	Share of profit		3 108	3 108
			£3 630	£3 716				£3 630	£3 716
					1972				
					Jan. 1	Balances	b/d	1 868	2 020

*Indicates result of calculation.

2. **Capital Accounts**

			Robinson £	Jones £			Robinson £	Jones £
19 . .					19 . . Dec. 31	Balances	11 500	9 400

Current Accounts

			Robinson £	Jones £				Robinson £	Jones £
19 . .					19 . .				
Dec. 31	Cash		3 000		Dec. 31	Salary			4 000
	Balances	c/d	1 050	8 050		½ Share of Profit	T	4 050	4 050
			£4 050	£8 050				£4 050	£8 050
					Jan. 1	Balances	b/d	1 050	8 050

Profit and Loss Appropriation Account

			£	£				£
19 . .				4 000	19 . .	Net Trading		
Dec. 31	Partners' Salary Share of Profit:	T			Dec. 31	Profit	b/d	12 100
	Robinson, ½ Share		4 050					
	Jones, ½ Share		4 050					
				8 100				
				£12 100				£12 100

Balance Sheet
as at 31st December, 19..
(Claims side only)

Claims	£	£	Assets	£	£
Capital Accounts					
Robinson	11 500				
Jones	9 400				
		20 900			
Current Accounts					
Robinson:					
½ Share of Profit	4 050				
Less Drawings	3 000				
		1 050			
Jones:					
½ Share of Profit	4 050				
Add Salary	4 000				
		8 050			

3

Capital Accounts

19..			Brown £	Tomlinson £	19..		Brown £	Tomlinson £
					Dec. 31	Balances	10 000·00	4 000·00

Current Account—Brown

19..			Months	Interest £	£	19..			£
Mar. 1	Cash		10	16·67	200·00	Dec. 31	Interest on		
Aug. 1	,,		5	8·33	200·00		Capital		1 000·00
						31	½ Share of		
Dec. 31	Interest				25·00		Profit	T	2 327·50
31	Balance	c/d			2 902·50				
					£3 327·50				£3 327·50
						Jan. 1	Balance	b/d	2 902·50

Current Account—Tomlinson

19..			Months	Interest £	£	19..			£
April 1	Cash		9	15·00	200·00	Dec. 31	Interest on		
July 1	,,		6	10·00	200·00		Capital		400·00
Oct. 1	,,		3	5·00	200·00	31	½ Share of		
Dec. 31	Interest				30·00		Profit	T	2 327·50
31	Balance	c/d			2 097·50				
					£2 727·50				£2 727·50
						Jan. 1	Balance	b/d	2 097·50

Profit and Loss Appropriation Account

19 . . Dec. 31			£	£	19 . . Dec. 31			£	£
	Interest on Capital:					Net Trading Profit	b/d		6 000·00
	Brown		1 000·00			Interest on Drawings:			
	Tomlinson		400·00			Brown		25·00	
				1 400·00		Tomlinson		30·00	
	Share of Profit:	T							55·00
	Brown, ½ Share		2 327·50						
	Tomlinson, ½ Share		2 327·50						
				4 655·00					
				£6 055·00					£6 055·00

Balance Sheet
as at 31st December, 19 . .
(Claims side only)

CLAIMS				ASSETS	£
Capital Accounts					
Brown		10 000·00			
Tomlinson		4 000·00			
			14 000·00		
Current Accounts					
Brown:					
½ Share of Profit		2 327·50			
Add Interest on Capital		1 000·00			
		3 327·50			
Less Drawings	400·00				
,, Interest on Drawings	25·00				
		425·00			
			2 902·50		
Tomlinson:					
½ Share of Profit		2 327·50			
Add Interest on Capital		400·00			
		2 727·50			
Less Drawings	600·00				
,, Interest on Drawings	30·00				
		630·00			
			2 097·50		

4 Similar to **2**.

Profit for division		£10 148·32
Interest on Capital:	Toogood	£12 00·00
	Waring	£800·00
Interest on Drawings:	Toogood	—
	Waring	£18·32
Current Accounts:	Toogood (Cr.)	£6 274·16
	Waring (Cr.)	£5 855·84

Capital Accounts

Date		A. Ajayi £	B. Ajayi £	Date		A. Ajayi £	B. Ajayi £
19..				19.. Jan. 1	Balances	4 000	3 000
				June 30	Cash	1 000	

Current Accounts

Date		A. Ajayi £	B. Ajayi £	Date		£	A. Ajayi £	B. Ajayi £
19.. Jan. 1	Balance	72		19.. Jan. 1	Balance			100
Jan. 1/Dec. 31	Cash: Drawings	3 650	3 650	Dec. 31	Salary			300
	Balance c/d	763			Interest on Capital:			
					A. Ajayi	160		
					,, ,,	20		
					B. Ajayi			
					Share of Profit		180	120
					Balance		4 305	2 583
					Balance c/d			547
		£4 485	£3 650				£4 485	£3 650
Jan. 1	Balance b/d		547	Jan. 1	Balance b/d		763	

5

Appropriation Account
for year ended 31st December, 19 . .

	£	£			£	£
Partners' Salaries Account:			Net Trading Profit	b/d	7 188	
B. Ajayi		300	Add Salary (wrongly			
Interest on Capital:			deducted)		300	
A. Ajayi		180				7 488
B. Ajayi		120				
Share of Profit:						
A. Ajayi	4 305					
B. Ajayi	2 583					
		6 888				
		£7 488				£7 488

6

Dickson's Capital Account

19 . .			£	19 . .			£
Dec. 31	Balance	c/d	2 000	Jan. 1	Balance	b/d	1 000
				July 1	Cash		600
				Dec. 31	Current A/c		400
			£2 000				£2 000
				Jan. 1	Balance	b/d	2 000

Dickson's Current Account

19 . .			£	19 . .			£
Dec. 31	Cash: Drawings		520	Jan. 1	Balance	b/d	300
31	Interest on Drawings		13	Dec. 31	Interest on Capital		65
31	Transferred to Capital A/c		400	31	Interest on Current A/c		15
31	Balance		1 497	31	Share of Profit ⅛ of £16 400		2 050
			£2 430				£2 430
				Jan. 1	Balance	b/d	1 497

7

Capital Accounts

		A £	B £	C £		19..		A £	B £	C £
19..						Dec. 31	Balances	10 000	8 000	6 000

Current Accounts

			A £	B £	C £		19..			A £	B £	C £
Dec. 31	Cash		4 200	3 000	5 000		Jan. 1	Balances				
31	Balances	c/d	3 450	2 233			Dec. 31	Salaries		500	200	350
							31	Interest on Capital		600	600	300
							31	Share of Profit, $\frac{1}{2}$ $\frac{1}{3}$ $\frac{1}{6}$		500	400	
								,, ,, ,,		6 050	4 033	2 017
								Balance	c/d			2 333
			£7 650	£5 233	£5 000					£7 650	£5 233	£5 000
Jan. 1	Balance	b/d			2 333		Jan. 1	Balances	b/d	3 450	2 233	

Capital Accounts

		X £	Y £	Z £
19..				
Jan. 1	Balances	4 000·00	3 000·00	1 000·00

Current Accounts

		X £	Y £	Z £			X £	Y £	Z £
19..					19..				
Jan. 1	Balances		50·00	100·00	Jan. 1	Balance	250·00		
Dec. 31	Drawings	1 300·00	925·00	1 200·00	Dec. 31	Salary			750·00
31	Balances c/d	150·80	145·80	28·40		Commission			58·00
						Interest on Capital	320·00	240·00	80·00
						Share of Profit, $\frac{2}{5}$ $\frac{2}{5}$ $\frac{1}{5}$	880·80	880·80	440·40
		£1 450·80	£1 120·80	£1 328·40			£1 450·80	£1 120·80	£1 328·40
					Jan. 1	Balances b/d	150·80	145·80	28·40

8

Profit and Loss Appropriation Account

19.. Dec. 31		£	£	19.. Dec. 31		£
	Salary Z		750·00		Net Trading Profit	3 650·00
	Commission Z:					
	Profit	3 650·00				
	Deduct Salary	750·00				
	2% Commission on	2 900·00	58·00			
	Interest on Capital:					
	X	320·00				
	Y	240·00				
	Z	80·00				
			640·00			
	Share of Profit					
	X = $\frac{2}{5}$	880·80				
	Y = $\frac{2}{5}$	880·80				
	Z = $\frac{1}{5}$	440·40				
			2 202·00			
			£3 650·00			£3 650·00

9   **Trading and Profit and Loss Account**
for year ended 31st December, 19..

		£	£			£
Stock, 1st January			23 170	Sales		86 730
Purchases			73 280			
			96 450			
Less Stock, 31st December			28 850			
			67 600			
Gross Profit	c/d		19 130			
			£86 730			£86 730
General Expenses		4 620		Gross Profit	b/d	19 130
Less Insurance Prepaid		360		Discounts		
			4 260	Received		290
Repairs to Premises			1 500			
Bad Debts			500			
Discounts Allowed			1 360			
Depreciation:						
Fixtures and Fittings			350			
Net Trading Profit	c/d		11 450			
			£19 420			£19 420
Interest on Capital:				Net Trading		
Copping		500		Profit	b/d	11 450
Watts		250				
			750			
Salary: Watts			2 500			
Share of Profit:						
Copping, $\frac{1}{2}$ Share		4 100				
Watts, $\frac{1}{2}$ Share		4 100				
			8 200			
			£11 450			£11 450

Balance Sheet
as at 31st December, 19 . .

CLAIMS	£	£	ASSETS	£	£	£
Capital Accounts			*Fixed Assets*			
Copping	10 000		Freehold Premises		25 000	
Watts	5 000		Fixtures and			
		15 000	Fittings	3 500		
			Less Depreciation	350		
Current Accounts					3 150	
Copping:						28 150
Share of Profit	4 100					
Add Interest on			*Current Assets*			
Capital	500		Stock, 31st Dec.		28 850	
	———		Debtors		31 180	
	4 600		Insurance Prepaid		360	
Less Drawings	2 500		Cash in hand		860	
		2 100				61 250
Watts:						
Share of Profit	4 100					
Add Interest on						
Capital	250					
,, Salary	2 500					
	———					
	6 850					
Less Drawings	4 000					
		2 850				
Current Liabilities						
Creditors	28 740					
Bank Overdraft	40 710					
		69 450				
		£89 400				£89 400

(*Note:* Continued on KEY page 156)

10

Trial Balance of Carrick and Furgus
31st March, 19.2

	£	£		£	£
Current Accounts (or Drawings):			Capital Accounts:		
Carrick	1 200		Carrick	20 000	
Furgus	600		Furgus	2 250	
		1 800			22 250
Factory Premises		9 000	Sales		53 944
Machinery		5 000	Rent Receivable		150
Fixtures and Fittings		400	Discounts Received		121
Factory Wages		13 397	Creditors		4 392
Stock, 31st March, 19.1		3 763			
Purchases		34 118			
Factory Power		1 592			
Telephone		177			
Expenses		849			
Salaries		2 479			
Discounts Allowed		461			
Bad Debts		158			
Debtors		5 649			
Cash at Bank		1 645			
Cash in hand		369			
		£80 857			£80 857
Stock at 31st March, 19.2		6 545			

Trading and Profit and Loss Account
for year ended 31st March, 19.2

		£			£
Stock, 1st April, 19.1		3 763	Sales		53 944
Purchases		34 118			
		37 881			
Less Stock, 31st March, 19.2		6 545			
		31 336			
Factory Wages		13 397			
Factory Power		1 592			
Depreciation:					
Machinery		1 000			
Cost of Sales		47 325			
Gross Profit	c/d	6 619			
		£53 944			£53 944
Salaries		2 479	Gross Profit	b/d	6 619
Expenses		849	Rent Receivable		150
Telephone		177	Discounts Received		121
Depreciation:					
Fixtures and Fittings		100			
Bad Debts		158			
Provision for Bad Debts		102			
Discounts Allowed		461			
Net Trading Profit	c/d	2 564			
		£6 890			£6 890
Share of Profit:			Net Trading Profit	b/d	2 564
Carrick, ¾ Share		1 923			
Furgus, ¼ Share		641			
		£2 564			£2 564

Balance Sheet
as at 31st March, 19.2

CLAIMS	£	£		ASSETS	£	£	£
Capital Accounts				*Fixed Assets*			
Carrick	20 000			Freehold Premises		9 000	
Furgus	2 250			Machinery at Cost	10 000		
		22 250		*Less* Accumulated			
Current Accounts				Depreciation	6 000		
Carrick:						4 000	
Share of Profit	1 923			Fixtures and			
Less Drawings	1 200			Fittings	800		
		723		*Less* Accumulated			
Furgus:				Depreciation	500		
Share of Profit	641					300	
Less Drawings	600						13 300
		41					
Current Liabilities				*Current Assets*			
Creditors		4 392		Stock, 31st March.			
				19.2		6 545	
				Debtors	5 649		
				Less Provisions for			
				Bad Debts	102		
						5 547	
				Cash at Bank		1 645	
				Cash in hand		369	
							14 106
		£27 406					£27 406

11

Trading and Profit and Loss Account
for the year ended 31st March, 1980

	£	£		£
Opening Stock		3 209	Sales	32 010
Purchases		23 015		
		26 224		
Less Closing Stock		3 004		
Cost of Goods Sold		23 220		
To Gross Profit		8 790		
		£32 010		£32 010
Wages and Salaries		2 154		
Rent		1 340	Gross Profit	8 790
Motor Lorry and Van			Discount Received	1 021
expenses		1 148		
Discounts allowed		850		
General Expenses		170		
Insurance		168		
Lighting and Heating		161		
Rates		160		
Printing and Stationery		155		
Bad Debts		80		
Provision for bad debts		75		
Depreciation:				
Motor Lorry and				
Van	400			
Furniture and				
Fittings	100	500		
		6 961		
Net Profit				
William	1 425			
James	1 425			
		2 850		
		£9 811		£9 811

(*Note:* Continued on KEY page 160)

Balance Sheet of William and James
as at 31st March, 1980

	£	£		£	£
Capital Accounts			*Fixed Assets*		
William	3 500		Motor Lorry and Van		
James	3 500		cost	2 000	
		7 000	*Less* Depreciation	400	
Current Accounts					1 600
William Howard	250		Furniture and Fittings		
James Howard	274		at Cost	700	
		524	*Add* Additions made		
		7 524	during year: Conv.		
			heater	32	
				732	
			Less Depreciation	100	
					632
					2 232
Current Liabilities			*Current Assets*		
Sundry Creditors:			Stock in Trade	3 004	
Trade Creditors	3 309		Sundry Debtors:		
Accruals:			Trade Debtors	3 500	
Rent	160		*Less* Provisions for		
Motor Van			bad debts	175	
Repairs	38			3 325	
	198		*Add* Prepayment		
		3 507	Rates	40	
				3 365	
			Cash at bank	2 430	
					8 799
		£11 031			£11 031

Current Accounts

1980			William £	James £	1980			William £	James £
Mar. 31	Drawings		1 175	1 151	Mar. 31	Share of Profit		1 425	1 425
31	Balances	c/d	250	274					
			£1 425	£1 425				£1 425	£1 425
					Apr. 1	Balances	b/d	250	274

12   **Profit and Loss Appropriation Account**
                          for half-year ended 30th June, 19..

	£	£		£
Interest on Capital:			Net Trading	
M.	150		Profit	3 126
L.	100			
		250		
Bonus to M.		250		
Share of Profit:				
M.	1 313			
L.	1 313			
		2 626		
		£3 126		£3 126

Balance Sheet
as at 30th June, 19..

CLAIMS	£	£	£	ASSETS	£	£	£
Capital Accounts				*Fixed Assets*			
M.		6 000		Freehold			
L.		4 000		Property		8 000	
			10 000	Furniture and			
Current Accounts				Equipment		475	
M.							8 475
Balance	300			*Current Assets*			
Interest on				Stock, 30th June		2 705	
Capital	150			Debtors	2 475		
Bonus	250			*Less* Provision			
Share of Profit	1 313			for Bad Debts	100		
	2 013					2 375	
Less Drawings	1 850			Advertising			
		163		Prepaid		800	
L.:				Cash in hand			
Balance	250			and at Bank		2 335	
Interest on							8 215
Capital	100						
Share of Profit	1 313						
	1 663						
Less Drawings	1 250						
		413					
			576				
Long-Term							
Liabilities							
Mortgage on							
Freehold							
Property			3 500				
Current Liabilities							
Creditors:							
Trade		2 510					
Expense		104					
			2 614				
			£16 690				£16 690

Note:
M. has been given precedence over L. because the partner with the greatest capital is
usually the senior partner.

13(*a*)

Profit and Loss Appropriation Account
for year ended 30th September, 19..

	£	£		£
Interest on Capital:			Net Trading Profit	4 369
F. Winter	390			
G. Frost	330			
		720		
Interest on Loan:				
F. Winter		175		
Share of Profit:				
F. Winter	1 737			
G. Frost	1 737			
		3 474		
		£4 369		£4 369

Balance Sheet
as at 30th September, 19..

CLAIMS	£	£	£	ASSETS	£	£	£
Capital Accounts				Goodwill			2 000
F. Winter		6 500		*Fixed Assets*			
G. Frost		5 500		Furniture and			
			12 000	Equipment			740
Current Accounts							
F. Winter:				*Current Assets*			
Balance	40			Stock, 30th Sept.		5 980	
Interest on				Debtors	5 490		
Capital	390			*Less* Provision	170		
Interest on						5 320	
Loan	175			Cash in hand			
Share of Profit	1 737			and at Bank		3 169	
	2 342						14 469
Less Drawings	2 300						
		42					
G. Frost:							
Balance	30						
Interest on							
Capital	330						
Share of Profit	1 737						
	2 097						
Less Drawings	2 000						
		97					
			139				
Long-Term							
Liabilities							
Loan Account:							
F. Winter			2 500				
Current Liabilities							
Creditors			2 570				
			£17 209				£17 209

13(*b*) (i)
         (ii) } See page 345.
         (iii)

Chapter 35   Exercises

1

Dr.			Cash Book Extract			*Cr.*
19..		£	19..			£
	Bentley:					
	Capital	1 000				

Capital: Bentley

19..			£	19..			£
					Cash		1 000

The premium is paid directly, *i.e.* privately, by Bentley, to the partners. No entry needed.

2

Dr.			Cash Book			*Cr.*
19..		£	19..			£
	Jackson:			Thomas:		
	Capital	1 000		Current A/c	500
	Premium	1 000		James:		
				Current A/c	500

Capital: Jackson

19..			£	19..			£
					Cash		1 000

Premium: Jackson

19..		£	19..			£
	Current			Cash		1 000
	Accounts:					
	Thomas	500				
	James	500				
		£1 000				£1 000

Current Accounts

19..		Thomas £	James £	19..		Thomas £	James £
	Cash	500	500		Premium: Jackson	500	500

3

Capital Accounts

		Wise £	Wisdom £	Woolley £
	Balances	30 000	20 000	
	Cash			15 000
	Premium: Woolley	6 000	4 000	

Premium: Woolley

		£				£
Capital: Wise		6 000	Cash			10 000
Wisdom		4 000				
		£10 000				£10 000

Dr.	**Cash Book Extract**					Cr.
Woolley:						£
Capital	15 000					
Premium	10 000					

4

Dr.		**Cash Book Extract**				Cr.
19..		£	19..			£
	Williams:					
	Capital	3 000				
	Premium	1 000				

Premium: Williams

19..		£	19..		£
	Capital Accounts:			Cash	1 000
	West	500			
	Wilson	500			
		£1 000			£1 000

Capital Accounts

West £	Wilson £	Williams £			West £	Wilson £	Williams £
			Balances	b/d	3 000	3 000	
			Cash				3 000
			Premium:				
			Jackson		500	500	
					£3 500	£3 500	£3 000

5 Similar to **4**.

6

Dr.				Cash Book Extract			Cr.
19 . .			£	19 . .			£
	Denton:						
	Capital		2 000				

Goodwill

19 . .			£	£	19 . .		£	£
	Capital							
	Accounts:	J						
	Caton		1 000					
	Coulter		1 000	2 000				

Capital Accounts

Caton £	Coulter £	Denton £			Caton £	Coulter £	Denton £
			Balances	b/d	4 000	4 000	
			Cash				2 000
			Goodwill	J	1 000	1 000	
					£5 000	£5 000	£2 000

Journal

		Dr.	Cr.
19 . .		£	£
	Goodwill	2 000	
	Capital Accounts:		
	Caton £1 000 ⎫		2 000
	Coulter £1 000 ⎭		
	Goodwill Account raised and transferred		
	to Capital Accounts in equal shares		

Future profit sharing ratio: Caton $\frac{5}{12}$, Coulter $\frac{5}{12}$, Denton $\frac{2}{12}$.

7 Similar to **6**.

8

Dr.				Cash Book Extract					Cr.
19..			£	19..					£
	C's Capital		3 000						
	C's Premium		1 000						

C's Premium Account

19..			£	£	19..			£
	Capital Accounts:	T				Cash	CB	1 000
	A: $\frac{2}{3}$ Share		666					
	B: $\frac{1}{3}$ Share		334					
				1 000				

Goodwill

19..			£	£	19..			£
	Capital Accounts:	J						
	A: $\frac{2}{3}$ Share		5 334					
	B: $\frac{1}{3}$ Share		2 666					
				8 000				

Capital Accounts

19..			A £	B £	C £	19..			A £	B £	C £
							Balances	b/d	6 000	3 000	
							C's Premium	T	666	334	
							Cash	CB			3 000
							Goodwill	J	5 334	2 666	
									£12 000	£6 000	£3 000

9

Capital Accounts

19..			£ A	£ B	19.. Jan. 1		£ A	£ B
						Balances	10 000	3 000
						Goodwill	6 000	

Appropriation Account (1)

	£	£		£
Interest on Capital:			Net Trading	
A 5% on £10 000	500		Profit	2 600
B 5% on £3 000	150			
		650		
Share of Profit:				
A $\frac{2}{3}$ Share	1 300			
B $\frac{1}{3}$ Share	650			
		1 950		
		£2 600		£2 600

Appropriation Account (2)

	£	£		£
Interest on Capital:			Net Trading	
A 5% on £16 000	800		Profit	2 600
B 5% on £3 000	150			
		950		
Share of Profit:				
A $\frac{2}{3}$ Share	1 100			
B $\frac{1}{3}$ Share	550			
		1 650		
		£2 600		£2 600

Chapter 36   Exercises

1

Dr.			Cash Book			Cr.
19 . .		£	19 . .		£	£
	Realisation			Creditors		1 456
	of Assets	11 441		Loan Account		1 000
				Capital Accounts:		
				McArthur	5 591	
				Dickson	3 394	
						8 985
		£11 441				£11 441

Capital Accounts

19 . .		McArthur £	Dickson £	19 . .		McArthur £	Dickson £
	Cash	5 591	3 394		Balances	5 000	3 000
					Profit on		
					Realisation	591	394
		£5 591	£3 394			£5 591	£3 394

2

Dr.					Cash Book			Cr.
19..			£	19..			£	£
	Balance		700·00		Creditors			17 600·00
	Realisation				Realisation			
	(proceeds of				Account			
	sale of				(Dissolution			
	assets)		43 500·00		Expenses)			180·00
					Capital			
					Accounts:			
					Adams		17 613·30	
					Bates		8 806·70	
								26 420·00
			£44 200·00					£44 200·00

Capital Accounts

19..		Adams £	Bates £	19..			Adams £	Bates £
	Realisa-tion A/c Share of Loss ⅔ and ⅓	5 386·70	2 693·30		Balances	b/d	23 000·00	11 500·00
	Cash	17 613·30	8 806·70					
		23 000·00	11 500·00				23 000·00	11 500·00

Creditors

19..			£	19..			£
	Cash		17 600·00		Balance		18 000·00
	Discount trans-ferred to Realisation Account		400·00				
			£18 000·00				£18 000·00

Realisation Account

19 . .			£	19 . .			£
Assets transferred	J		51 800·00	Cash: Proceeds of sale of assets	CB		43 500·00
Cash: Dissolution Expenses	CB		180·00	Discounts Received transferred from creditors	J		400·00
				Balance	c/d		8 080·00
			£51 980·00				£51 980·00
Balance	b/d		8 080·00	Capital Accounts: Share of Loss transferred:	T		
				Adams, $\frac{2}{3}$			5 386·70
				Bates, $\frac{1}{3}$			2 693·30
			£8 080·00				£8 080·00

3

Realisation Account

19 . .			£	19 . .			£
Assets transferred	J		7 800	Capital: A. Brown (Furniture taken over)	J		1 450
Cash: Dissolution Expenses	CB		91				
Balances	c/d		84	Cash (Proceeds of sale of assets and debtors' payments)			6 525
			£7 975				£7 975
Capital Accounts: Share of Profit transferred:				Balance	b/d		84
A. Brown, $\frac{2}{3}$ Share			56				
W. Green, $\frac{1}{3}$ Share			28				
			£84				£84

Bank Balance transferred to Capital Accounts: A. Brown £2 406; W. Green £1 928.

4 Similar to **2** and **3**.
Realisation Account Loss: A's $\frac{1}{2}$ Share £2 500; B's $\frac{1}{2}$ Share £2 500; Bank Balance transferred to Capital Accounts: A £17 500; B £12 500.

Chapter 37   Exercises

1 (*a*) See pages 396, 400 of textbook.
   (*b*) See pages 402–4 of textbook.

2 (*a*) See page 396 of textbook.
   (*b*) See page 397 of textbook.

3 Private Company, pages 397–8 of textbook.
   Public Company, pages 395–6 of textbook.

4 See page 404.

5 (*a*) See page 405.
   (*b*) See page 406.

Chapter 38   Exercises

1

	Journal	Dr.	Cr.
19..		£	£
July 16	Applications and Allotment	5 000 000	
	Ordinary Share Capital		5 000 000
	£0·15 per share on application and		
	£0·85 per share on allotment on		
	5 000 000 shares of £1 each by resolution		
	of the directors		

Cash Book (Debit side only)

			£
19..			
July 1	Application and Allotment Accounts Instalment of £0·15 per share on 5 000 000 shares on application		750 000
16	Application and Allotment Accounts £0·85 per share on 5 000 000 shares on allotment		4 250 000

Application and Allotment Account

19.. July 16	Ordinary Share Capital A/c	J	£ 5 000 000	19.. July 1 16	Cash ,,	CB CB	£ 750 000 4 250 000
			£5 000 000				£5 000 000

Ordinary Share Capital

19..			£	19.. July 16	Application and Allotment A/c	J	£ 5 000 000

Balance Sheet

CLAIMS	£	£	
Authorised Capital			
8 000 000 Ordinary Shares of £1 each	8 000 000		
Issued Capital			
5 000 000 Ordinary Shares of £1 each		5 000 000	

2 Similar to **1**.

3

	Journal	Dr.	Cr.
19..		£	£
Oct. 1	Application and Allotment	100 000	
	Ordinary Share Capital		100 000
	£1·25 per share on application and		
	£3·75 per share on allotment on		
	20 000 ordinary shares of £10 each by		
	resolution of the directors		
Nov. 1	First and Final Call Account	100 000	
	Ordinary Share Capital Account		100 000
	£5·00 per share on 20 000 shares by		
	the terms of the issue		

Cash Book

(Debit side only)

19..			£	
Oct. 1	Application and Allotment Account Instalment of £1·25 per share on 20 000 shares		25 000	
	Application and Allotment Account Instalment of £3·75 per share on 20 000 shares		75 000	
Nov. 1	First and Final Call Account Call money of £5·00 per share on 20 000 shares		100 000	

Application and Allotment Account

19.. Oct. 1	Ordinary Share Capital A/c	J	£ 100 000	19.. Oct. 1 1	Cash ,,	CB CB	£ 25 000 75 000
			£100 000				£100 000

First and Final Call Account

19.. Nov. 1	Ordinary Share Capital A/c	J	£ 100 000	19.. Nov. 1	Cash	CB	£ 100 000

Ordinary Share Capital

19..			£	19.. Oct. 1	Balance		£ 1 000 000
					Application and Allotment	J	100 000
				Nov. 1	First and Final Call		100 000

Balance Sheet

(Claims side only)

CLAIMS *Authorised Capital and Issued Capital* 120 000 Ordinary Shares of £10 each, fully paid	£ 1 200 000	

4 Similar to **3**.

5 Similar to previous questions. Add only Second and Final Call Account.

Second and Final Call

19.. June	Ordinary Share Capital	J	£ 1 000 000	19.. June 30	Cash	CB	£ 1 000 000

Ordinary Share Capital

19..			£	19..			£
				Mar. 30	Application and Allotment	J	2 000 000
				April 30	First Call	J	1 000 000
				June 30	Second and Final Call	J	1 000 000

Balance Sheet
(Claims side only)

	£	£	
CLAIMS			
Authorised Capital			
5 000 000 Ordinary Shares of £1 each	5 000 000		
Issued Capital			
4 000 000 Ordinary Shares of £1 each fully paid		4 000 000	

6 Similar to **5**.

7 Similar to **5** and **6**, except the following:

Second and Final Call

19.. Mar.	Ordinary Share Capital	J	£ 30 000	19.. Mar. 15 31	Cash Balance	CB c/d	£ 29 500 500
			£30 000				£30 000
April 1	Balance (2 000 shares H. Watson Final Call unpaid)	b/d	500				

Ordinary Share Capital

19 . .			£	19 . .			£
				Jan. 1	Application and Allotment	J	60 000
				Feb. 15	First Call	J	30 000
				Mar. 15	Second and Final Call	J	30 000

Balance Sheet
(Claims side only)

CLAIMS	£	£
Authorised Capital		
150 000 Ordinary Shares of £1 each	150 000	
Issued Capital		
120 000 Ordinary Shares of £1 each fully called	120 000	
Less Calls in arrear	500	
		119 500

8 Similar to **7.**

9

Cash Book
(Debit side only)

19 . .		£
Oct. 1	*Preference Shares* Application and Allotment £0·15 per share on application	6 000
15	Application and Allotment £0·35 per share on allotment	14 000
Dec. 1	First and Final Call £0·50 per share	20 000
Oct. 1	*Ordinary Shares* Application and Allotment £0·15 per share on application	7 500
15	Application and Allotment £0·35 per share on allotment	17 500
Dec. 1	First and Final Call £0·50 per share	25 000

Continue with two separate but identical sets of entries (except for the amounts), respectively for 6% Preference Shares and Ordinary Shares.

The following are the 6% Preference Shares Accounts:

Application and Allotment 6% Preference Shares

19.. Oct. 15	Preference Shares Capital A/c	J	£ 20 000	19.. Oct. 1 15	Cash ,,	CB CB	£ 6 000 14 000
			£20 000				£20 000

First and Final Call 6% Preference Shares

19.. Dec. 1	Preference Shares Capital A/c	J	£ 20 000	19.. Dec. 1	Cash	CB	£ 20 000

6% Preference Share Capital

19..			£	19.. Oct. 15 Dec. 1	Application and Allotment First and Final Call	J J	£ 20 000 20 000

Balance Sheet
(Claims side only)

CLAIMS	£	£
Authorised Capital		
40 000 6% Preference		
Shares of £1 each	40 000	
60 000 Ordinary Shares		
of £1 each	60 000	
	£100 000	
Issued Capital		
40 000 6% Preference		
Shares of £1 each,		
fully paid	40 000	
50 000 Ordinary Shares		
of £1 each, fully paid	50 000	
		90 000

10 Showing Ordinary Share accounts only. Similar entries for Preference Shares needed.

Cash Book
(Debit side only)

			£
19..	*Ordinary Shares*		
Mar. 1	Application and Allotment £0·12½ per share on application		3 750
15	Application and Allotment £0·37½ per share on allotment		11 250
15	Calls in advance (1 000 shares at £0·50)		500

LEDGER
Application and Allotment Ordinary Shares

19..			£	19..			£
Mar. 15	Ordinary Share Capital	J	15 000	Mar. 1	Cash	CB	3 750
				15	,,	CB	11 250
			£15 000				£15 000

Calls in Advance, Ordinary Shares

19..			£	19..			£
				Mar. 15	Cash		500

Ordinary Share Capital

19..			£	19..			£
				Mar. 15	Application and Allotment	J	15 000

Balance Sheet
(Claims side only)

CLAIMS	£	£	
Authorised Capital			
4 600 000 6% Preference			
Shares of £1 each	4 600 000		
40 000 Ordinary Shares of			
£10 each	400 000		
	£5 000 000		
Issued Capital			
4 600 000 6% Preference			
Shares of £1 each			
(£0·50 per share paid)		2 300 000	
30 000 Ordinary Shares of			
£10 each (£5 per			
share paid)	150 000		
Add Calls in Advance	5 000		
		155 000	

11 See pages 347 and 411.

Chapter 39   Exercises

1

	Journal		Dr.	Cr.
19 . .			£	£
June 15	Applications and Allotment		300 000	
	Ordinary Share Capital			200 000
	Premium on Ordinary Shares			100 000
	£0·15 per share on application and			
	£0·60 per share, including £0·25 per			
	share premium on allotment of 400 000			
	Ordinary Shares			
July 15	First and Final Call Account		200 000	
	Ordinary Share Capital			200 000
	First and Final Call of £0·50 per			
	share on 400 000 shares			

Cash Book
(Debit side only)

19..			£
June 1	Application and Allotment Account £0·15 per share on 400 000 shares		60 000
15	Application and Allotment Account £0·60 per share (including £0·25 premium) on 400 000 shares		240 000
July 15	First and Final Call Account £0·50 per share on 400 000 shares		200 000

Application and Allotment Account

19..			£	19..			£
June 15	Ordinary Share Capital	J	200 000	June 1	Cash	CB	60 000
	Premium on Shares	J	100 000	15	,,	CB	240 000
			£300 000				£300 000

First and Final Call Account

19..			£	19..			£
July 15	Ordinary Share Capital	J	200 000	July 15	Cash	CB	200 000

Ordinary Share Capital

19..			£	19..			£
				June 15	Application and Allotment	J	200 000
				July 15	First and Final Call	J	200 000

Premium on Ordinary Shares

19 . .			£	19 . . June 15	Application and Allot- ment	J	£ 100 000

Balance Sheet
(Claims side only)

CLAIMS	£	
Authorised and Issued Capital		
1 000 000 Ordinary Shares		
of £1 each fully paid	1 000 000	
Share Premium		
Premium on Ordinary		
Shares	100 000	

2 Similar to **1.**

First and Final Call Account

19 . .	Ordinary Share Capital		£ 10 000	19 . .	Cash Balance	 c/d	£ 9 750 250
			£10 000				£10 000
	Balance	b/d	250				

Balance Sheet
(Extract)

CLAIMS	£	ASSETS	£
Authorised and Issued Capital		*Current Assets*	
40 000 Ordinary Shares of £1		Cash	41 750
each fully called	40 000		
Less Calls in arrear	250		
	39 750		
Share Premium			
Premium on Ordinary Shares	2 000		

3

Journal		Dr.	Cr.
19..		£	£
Feb. 10	Application and Allotment (Ordinary Shares)	40 000·00	
	Ordinary Share Capital		30 000·00
	Premium on Ordinary Shares		10 000·00
	£0·12½ per share on application and £0·37½ per share on allotment, including premium of £0·12½ per share on 80 000 Ordinary Shares of £1 each		
10	Application and Allotment Account (Preference Shares)	16 875·00	
	6% Preference Share Capital		16 875·00
	£0·12½ per share on application and £0·25 per share on allotment on 45 000 Preference Shares of £1 each		
Mar. 15	First and Final Call (Ordinary Shares)	50 000·00	
	Ordinary Share Capital		50 000·00
	£0·62½ per share on 80 000 Ordinary Shares of £1 each		
15	First and Final Call (Preference Shares)	28 125·00	
	6% Preference Share Capital		28 125·00
	£0·62½ per share on 45 000 Preference Shares of £1 each		

Cash Book

(Debit side only)

19..		£	
Feb. 1	Application and Allotment (Ordinary Shares) £0·12½ on application	10 000·00	
1	Application and Allotment (6% Preference Shares) £0·12½ on application	5 625·00	
10	Application and Allotment (Ordinary Shares) £0·37½ on allotment	30 000·00	
10	Application and Allotment (6% Preference Shares) £0·25 on allotment	11 250·00	
Mar. 15	First and Final Call (Ordinary Shares	50 000·00	
15	First and Final Call (6% Preference Shares)	28 062·50	

Application and Allotment (Ordinary Shares)

19..			£	19..			£
Feb. 10	Ordinary Share Capital	J	30 000·00	Feb. 1 10	Cash ,,		10 000·00 30 000·00
	Premium on Ordinary Shares	J	10 000·00				
			£40 000·00				£40 000·00

First and Final Call (Ordinary Shares)

19..			£	19..		£
Mar. 15	Ordinary Share Capital	J	50 000·00	Mar. 15	Cash	50 000·00

Ordinary Share Capital

19..			£	19..		£
				Feb. 10	Application and Allotment	30 000·00
				Mar. 15	First and Final Call	50 000·00

Premium on Ordinary Shares

19..			£	19..		£
				Feb. 10	Application and Allotment	10 000·00

Application and Allotment (6% Preference Shares)

19..			£	19..			£
Feb. 10	Preference Share Capital	J	16 875·00	Feb. 1 10	Cash ,,		5 625·00 11 250·00
			£16 875·00				£16 875·00

First and Final Call (6% Preference Shares)

19..			£	19..			£
Mar. 15	Preference Share Capital	J	28 125·00	Mar. 15	Cash	c/d	28 062·50
				31	Balance		62·50
			£28 125·00				£28 125·00
April 1	Balance	b/d	62·50				

6% Preference Shares

19..			£	19..			£
				Feb. 10	Application and Allotment	J	16 875·00
				Mar. 15	First and Final Call	J	28 125·00

4

	Journal		*Dr.*	*Cr.*
19..			£	£
Jan. 17	Application and Allotment		1 500 000	
	Ordinary Share Capital			1 000 000
	Premium on Ordinary Shares			500 000
	£0·50 per share on 1 000 000 Ordinary Shares of £1 each on application and £1 per share, including £0·50 premium on allotment			

Dr.	**Cash Book**			*Cr.*
19..		£	19..		£
Jan. 1	Application and Allotment: Applications received at £0·50 per share	557 500	Jan. 17	Non-allottee's deposits returned	57 500
17	Application and Allotment: Allotment money received at £0·50 per share and premium at £0·50 per share	1 000 000			

Application and Allotment

19..			£	19..			£
Jan. 17	Ordinary Share Capital	J	1 000 000	Jan. 1	Cash	CB	557 500
17	Share Premium	J	500 000	17	,,,	CB	1 000 000
17	Cash: Deposits returned		57 500				
			£1 557 500				£1 557 500

Ordinary Share Capital

19..			£	19..			£
				Jan. 17	Application and Allotment	J	1 000 000

Premium on Ordinary Shares

19..			£	19..			£
				Jan. 17	Application and Allotment	J	500 000

5

	Journal		Dr.	Cr.
19..			£	£
June 15	Application and Allotment		20 000	
	Ordinary Share Capital			20 000
	£0·25 per share on application and £0·25 per share on allotment on 40 000 Ordinary Shares of £1 each			
Aug. 15	First and Final Call		18 000	
	Discount on Ordinary Shares		2 000	
	Ordinary Share Capital			20 000
	£0·45 per share on 40 000 Ordinary Shares of £1 each and the discount of 5%			

LEDGER
Discount on Ordinary Shares

19..			£	19..			£
Aug. 15	Ordinary Share Capital	J	2 000				

Ordinary Share Capital

19..			£	19..			£
				Jan. 1	Balance	b/d	80 000
				June 15	Application and Allotment	J	20 000
				Aug. 15	First and Final Call	J	18 000
				15	Discount on Shares	J	2 000
							£120 000

Balance Sheet
(Extract)

CLAIMS	£	ASSETS	£
Authorised and Issued Capital 120 000 Ordinary Shares of £1 each, fully paid	120 000	Discount on Ordinary Shares	2 000

6 Similar to **5**.

Chapter 40   Exercises

1

Journal

		Dr.	Cr.
19..		£	£
June 9	12% Debentures, Application and Allotment	100 000	
	12% Debentures		100 000
	£20 per debenture on application and £80 per debenture on allotment of 1 000 12% Debentures of £100 each on resolution of the Directors		

Cash Book
(Debit side only)

19..			£
June 1	12% Debentures Application and Allotment, Application moneys for 1 000 debentures at £20 each		20 000
9	12% Debentures Application and Allotment. Allotment moneys for 1 000 debentures at £80 each		80 000

LEDGER
12% Debentures Application and Allotment

19..			£	19..				£
June 9	12% Debentures	J	100 000	June 1	Cash	CB	20 000
				9	,,	CB	80 000

12% Debentures

19..			£	19..				£
				June 9	Application and Allotment	J	100 000

Balance Sheet
(Claims side only)

CLAIMS	£	£
Authorised and Issued Capital		
50 000 6% Preference Shares of £1 each fully paid	50 000	
100 000 Ordinary Shares of £1 each fully paid	100 000	
		150 000
Loan Capital		
1 000 12% Debentures of £100 each fully paid		100 000

2

Journal					Dr.	Cr.
19..					£	£
Jan. 1	11% Debentures, Application and Allotment				50 000	
	11% Debentures					50 000
	£20 per debenture on application and £30 per debenture on allotment of 1 000 11% Debentures of £100 each on resolution of the Directors					
Feb. 5	11% Debentures First and Final Call				50 000	
	11% Debentures					50 000
	£50 per debenture on 1 000 debentures of £100 each in accordance with terms of issue					

LEDGER
11% Debentures Application and Allotment

19..			£	19..			£
Jan. 5	11% Debentures	J	50 000	Jan. 1	Cash	CB	20 000
				5	,,	CB	30 000

11% Debentures First and Final Call

19..			£	19..			£
Feb. 5	11% Debentures	J	50 000	Feb. 5	Cash	CB	50 000

11% Debentures

19..			£	19..			£
				Jan. 5	Application and Allotment	J	50 000
				Feb. 5	First and Final Call	J	50 000

3

Journal					Dr.	Cr.
19..					£	£
Feb. 8	10% Debentures, Application and Allotment				105 000	
	10% Debentures					100 000
	Premium on Debentures					5 000
	£20 per debenture on application and £85 per debenture on allotment, including £5 per debenture premium on 1 000 10% Debentures of £100 each in accordance with Directors' resolution					

Cash Book
(Debit side only)

19..			£	
Feb. 1	10% Debenture Application and Allotment. Instalment of £20 per debenture on 1 000 debentures		20 000	
8	10% Debenture Application and Allotment. Instalment of £85 per debenture, including premium		85 000	

LEDGER

10% Debenture Application and Allotment

19..			£	19..			£
Feb. 8	10% Debentures	J	100 000	Feb. 1	Cash	CB	20 000
	Premium on 10% Debentures	J	5 000	8	,,	CB	85 000

10% Debentures

19..			£	19..			£
				Feb. 8	Application and Allotment	J	100 000

Premium on 10% Debentures

19..		£	19..			£
			Feb. 8	Application and Allotment	J	5 000

4 Similar to **3**.

5

Balance Sheet of Remington and Sons Ltd
(Extract)

CLAIMS	£	ASSETS	£
Loan Capital		*Discount on Debentures*	1 000
500 7% Debentures of £100 each fully paid	50 000	*Debenture Issue Expenses*	500
			1 500
		Current Assets	
		Cash	48 500

6 Journal entries Similar to **3.**

Dr.			**Cash Book**				*Cr.*
19..			£	19..			£
	Application and Allotment (13½% Debentures)		510 000		Debenture Issue Expenses Balance	c/d	16 000 494 000
			£510 000				£510 000
	Balance	b/d	494 000				

13½% Debentures Application and Allotment

19..			£	19..			£
	13½ Debentures Premium on 13½% Debentures	J J	500 000 10 000		Cash	CB	510 000

13½% Debentures

19..			£	19..			£
					Application and Allotment		500 000

Premium on 13½% Debentures

19..			£	19..			£
					Application and Allotment	J	10 000

Debenture Issue Expenses

19..			£	19..			£
	Cash	CB	16 000				

Balance Sheet of Jennings Stores Ltd
(Extract)

CLAIMS	£	ASSETS	£
Loan Capital		Debenture Issue Expenses	16 000
5 000 13½% Debentures of £100 each fully paid	500 000	*Current Assets*	
Premium on Debentures	10 000	Cash	494 000

Journal				Dr.	Cr.
				£	£
19.. Mar. 9	12% Debentures Application and Allotment 12% Debentures £20 per debenture on application and £40 per debenture on allotment of 1 000 debentures at £100 each			60 000	60 000
April 9	Debenture Discount 12% Debentures Discount of £2 per debenture on 1 000 12% Debentures issued at £98			2 000	2 000
9	12% Debentures First and Final Call 12% Debentures Final instalment of £38 each on 1 000 debentures by the conditions of issue			38 000	38 000

LEDGER
12% Debentures Application and Allotment

19.. Mar. 9	12% Debentures	J	£ 60 000	19.. Mar. 1 9	Cash ,,	CB CB	£ 20 000 40 000

12% Debentures

19..			£	19.. Mar. 9 April 9 9	Application and Allotment First and Final Call Debenture Discount	J J J	£ 60 000 38 000 2 000

12% Debentures First and Final Call

19.. April 9	12% Debentures	J	£ 38 000	19.. April 9	Cash	CB	£ 38 000

Debenture Discount

19.. April 9	12% Debentures	J	£ 2 000	19..			£

8 Similar to **7**.

Balance Sheet of Lawson's Limited

Claims	£	Assets	£
Loan Capital		*Discount on Debentures*	250 000
50 000 10% Debentures of		*Current Assets*	
£100 each fully paid	5 000 000	Cash	4 750 000

9

	Journal	Dr.	Cr.
19 . .		£	£
Mar. 31	(a) Provision for Bad Debts	30 000	
	Profit and Loss Account		30 000
	Provision written down		
	(b) Profit and Loss Account	30 000	
	Debenture Interest		30 000
	Interest on £1 000 000 of 6% Debenture		
	for six months		
	(c) Buildings	140 000	
	Purchases		75 000
	Wages		65 000
	Transfer of amounts relating to		
	expenditure on building an extension		
	to factory		

Chapter 41 Exercises

1 Alternative to textbook method. See below for textbook method.

Journal		Dr.	Cr.
19..		£	£
Dec. 31	Land and Buildings	3 800	
	Machinery and Plant	2 500	
	Fixtures and Fittings	416	
	Stock	4 891	
	Debtors	2 340	
	Goodwill	2 420	
	Provision for Bad Debts		117
	Creditors		1 250
	Vendors: Grace and Robins		15 000
	Assets and Liabilities acquired on		
	purchase of business	£16 367	£16 367
31	Vendor	14 000	
	6% Preference Share Capital		4 000
	Ordinary Share Capital		10 000
	Allotment of Preference and Ordinary		
	Shares (4 000 and 10 000, respectively),		
	to vendor, being part purchase price of		
	his business	£14 000	£14 000
31	Application and Allotment	5 000	
	Ordinary Share Capital		5 000
	Balance of the Ordinary Shares,		
	i.e. 5 000 issued to the public		

Dr.					**Cash Book**			Cr.
19..			£	19..				£
Feb. 28	Application and Allotment		5 000	Feb. 28	Vendors: Grace and Robins			1 000
				28	Preliminary Expenses			436
					Balance	c/d		3 564
			£5 000					£5 000
Mar. 1	Balance	b/d	3 564					

Balance Sheet of Grace and Co. Ltd
as at 28th February, 19..

CLAIMS	£	ASSETS	£	£	£
Registered Capital		Goodwill			2 420
15 000 6% Preference		*Fixed Assets*			
Shares of £1 each	15 000	Land and Buildings		3 800	
15 000 Ordinary Shares		Machinery and Plant		2 500	
of £1 each	15 000	Fixtures and Fittings		416	
	───			───	9 136
	30 000	*Current Assets*			
	═══	Stock, 28th February		4 891	
Issued Capital		Debtors	2 340		
4 000 6% Preference		*Less* Provision for			
Shares of £1 each		Bad Debts	117		
fully paid	4 000		───	2 223	
15 000 Ordinary Shares		Cash		3 564	
of £1 each fully paid	15 000			───	10 678
	───	*Preliminary Expenses*			436
	19 000				
Current Liabilities					
Creditors	1 250				
	───				───
	£20 250				£20 250
	═══				═══

1　Textbook method.

	Journal	Dr.	Cr.
19..		£	£
Dec. 31	Business Purchase	15 000	
	Vendors: Grace and Robins		15 000
	Purchase price of business		
31	Goodwill	250	
	Land and Buildings	3 100	
	Machinery and Plant	2 720	
	Fixtures and Fittings	416	
	Stock	4 891	
	Debtors	2 340	
	Business Purchase		13 717
	Assets acquired on purchase of business		
		£13 717	£13 717
31	Business Purchase	1 367	
	Creditors		1 250
	Provision for Bad Debts		117
	Liabilities taken over on purchase of		
	business	£1 367	£1 367
		£	£
31	Land and Buildings	700	
	Machinery and Plant		220
	Goodwill Account		480
	Revaluation of assets on purchase of		
	business		
		£700	£700

19 . .			
Dec. 31	Goodwill	2 650	
	Business Purchase		2 650
	Value of Goodwill acquired		
31	Vendor	14 000	
	6% Preference Share Capital		4 000
	Ordinary Share Capital		10 000
	Allotment of Preference and Ordinary		
	Shares (4 000 and 10 000, respectively)		
	to vendor, being part purchase price		
	of business		
		£14 000	£14 000
31	Application and Allotment	5 000	
	Ordinary Share Capital		5 000
	Balance of the Ordinary Shares,		
	i.e. 5 000, issued to the public		

LEDGER
Business Purchase

19 . .			£	19 . .			£
Dec. 31	Vendor		15 000	Dec. 31	Sundry Assets		13 717
	Sundry				Goodwill		
	Liabilities		1 367		(Balance)		2 650
			£16 367				£16 367

Goodwill

19 . .			£	19 . .			£
Dec. 31	Business			Dec. 31	Land and		
	Purchases		2 650		Buildings		
	Balance	J	250		and		
					Machinery		
					and Plant	J	480
					Balance	c/d	2 420
			£2 900				£2 900
Jan. 1	Balance	b/d	2 420				

Continue with Cash Book and Balance Sheet as on KEY pages 191–2.

2

Journal	Dr.	Cr.
19 . .	£	£
Patents and Trade Marks	8 000	
Freehold Works	75 000	
Plant and Machinery	31 000	
Stock	66 000	
Debtors	112 000	
Goodwill	20 000	
Creditors		12 000
Vendor		300 000
Assets and Liabilities acquired on purchase of business		
	£312 000	£312 000
Vendor	300 000	
7% Preference Share Capital		50 000
Ordinary Share Capital		50 000
9% Debenture Stock		100 000
Cash		100 000
Allotment of Preference and Ordinary Shares, and Debentures, together with cash in payment of business purchased from vendor		
	£300 000	£300 000
Cash	300 000	
7% Preference Share Capital		200 000
Ordinary Share Capital		100 000
Balances of Preference and Ordinary Shares (200 000 of each) issued to the public		
	£300 000	£300 000

Balance Sheet of Enterprise Ltd

CLAIMS	£		ASSETS	£	£
Authorised Capital			*Goodwill*		20 000
250 000 7% Preference			*Fixed Assets*		
Shares of £1 each	250 000		Patents and Trade		
500 000 Ordinary Shares			Marks	8 000	
of £0·50 each	250 000		Freehold Works	75 000	
	———		Plant and		
	£500 000		Machinery	31 000	
				———	114 000
Issued Capital			*Current Assets*		
250 000 7% Preference			Stock	66 000	
Shares of £1 each fully			Debtors	112 000	
paid	250 000		Cash at Bank	200 000	
300 000 Ordinary Shares of				———	378 000
£0·50 each fully paid	150 000				
	———				
	400 000				
Loan Capital					
9% Debentures	100 000				
Current Liabilities					
Sundry Creditors	12 000				
	———				———
	£512 000				£512 000

Note: If a Cash Book were shown, it would appear as follows:

Dr.				Cash Book			Cr.
19..			£	19..			£
	Preference				Vendor		100 000
	Share Capital		200 000		Balance	c/d	200 000
	Ordinary Share						
	Capital		100 000				
			———				———
			£300 000				£300 000
	Balance	b/d	200 000				

In this case, the 'Cash' item in the second Journal entry above would be omitted. The third entry in the Journal would not appear at all. Some examiners require candidates to show Journal entries *only* (no Cash Book).

Alternative Journal Entries	*Dr.*	*Cr.*
19..	£	£
Business Purchase	300 000	
Vendor		300 000
Purchase price of business		
Patents and Trade Marks	8 000	
Freehold Works	75 000	
Rent and Machinery	31 000	
Stock	66 000	
Debtors	112 000	
Goodwill	20 000	
Business Purchase		312 000
Assets acquired on purchase of business		
	£312 000	£312 000
Business Purchase	12 000	
Creditors		12 000
Liabilities taken over on purchase of business		

These three entries substitute the *first* Journal entry of the above alternative method (KEY page 194).

	Journal Opening Entries	*Dr.*	*Cr.*
19 . .		£	£
	Freehold Works	36 000	
	Machinery and Plant	37 860	
	Debtors	18 764	
	Stock	22 440	
	Cash in hand	976	
	Goodwill	20 000	
	Creditors		14 040
	Bank Loan		2 000
	Vendor		120 000
	Assets and Liabilities acquired on purchase of business		
		£136 040	£136 040
	Vendor	90 000	
	Preference Share Capital		50 000
	Ordinary Share Capital		40 000
	50 000 6% Preference Shares of £1 each, 40 000 Ordinary Shares of £1 each, given to vendor as part purchase price of business		
	Application and Allotment Preference Shares	50 000	
	6% Preference Shares Capital		50 000
	50 000 Preference Shares of £1 each transferred		
	Application and Allotment Ordinary Shares	60 000	
	Ordinary Shares Capital		60 000
	60 000 Ordinary Shares of £1 each transferred		

Dr.			**Cash Book**			*Cr.*
19 . .			£	19 . .		£
	Application and Allotment 6% Preference Shares		50 000		Vendor: Abel Chatenay	30 000
					Bank Loan	2 000
					Balance c/d	78 000
	Application and Allotment Ordinary Shares		60 000			
			£110 000			£110 000
	Balance	b/d	78 000			

Balance Sheet of Chatenays Ltd

CLAIMS	£	ASSETS	£	£
Authorised and Issued Capital		*Goodwill*		20 000
100 000 6% Preference		*Fixed Assets*		
Shares of £1 each fully		Freehold Works	36 000	
paid	100 000	Machinery and		
100 000 Ordinary Shares at		Plant	37 860	
£1 each fully paid	100 000		————	73 860
		Current Assets		
Current Liabilities		Stock	22 440	
Creditors	14 040	Debtors	18 764	
		Cash at Bank	78 000	
		Cash in hand	976	
			————	120 180
	————			————
	£214 040			£214 040

4

	Journal Opening Entries	Dr.	Cr.
19 ..		£	£
Jan. 1	Freehold Property	5 000	
	Machinery	3 250	
	Debtors	3 786	
	Cash at Bank	254	
	Cash in hand	10	
	Goodwill	5 000	
	Loan Account: J. Alpha		1 200
	Creditors		1 100
	Vendor: A. Alpha		15 000
	Assets and Liabilities acquired on		
	purchase of business		
		£17 300	£17 300
Jan. 1	Vendor	15 000	
	Ordinary Share Capital		15 000
	15 000 Ordinary Shares of £1 each		
	allotted to vendor as purchase price		
	of business		
Jan. 1	Loan Account: J. Alpha	1 200	
	Ordinary Share Capital		1 200
	1 200 Ordinary Shares of £1 each		
	allotted to J. Alpha in part payment		
	of Loan Account		

Dr.				**Cash Book**				Cr.
19 . .			£	19 . .				£
Jan. 1	Balance		254	Jan. 1	Balance		c/d	4 054
	Ordinary Share Capital (J. Alpha)		3 800					
			£4 054					£4 054
Jan. 1	Balance	b/d	4 054					

Balance Sheet of A. Alpha Ltd
as at 1st January, 19 . .

CLAIMS	£	ASSETS	£	£
Authorised and Issued Capital		Goodwill		5 000
20 000 Ordinary Shares of		*Fixed Assets*		
£1 each fully paid	20 000	Freehold Property	5 000	
		Machinery	3 250	
				8 250
				13 250
		Current Assets		
		Debtors	3 786	
		Cash at Bank	4 054	
		Cash in hand	10	
			7 850	
		Current Liabilities		
		Creditors	1 100	
		Working Capital		6 750
	£20 000			£20 000

5

		Journal		*Dr.*	*Cr.*
19 . .			£	£	£
Jan. 1	Plant			33 110·00	
	Furniture, etc.			18 090·00	
	Stock			54 910·00	
	Goodwill		33 300·00		
	Less excess of book value of				
	Assets over purchase price		4 410·00		
				28 890·00	
	Vendor, Joseph Andrews				135 000·00
	Assets acquired on purchase of business			£135 000·00	135 000·00

Dr.					Cash Book			Cr.

19 ..			£	19 ..				£
Jan. 16	Application and Allotment			Jan. 30	Vendor			50 000·00
			49 000·00	31	Vendor: Cash from his debtors, less 2½%			
30	Application and Allotment		49 000·00		commission			40 043·25
31	Vendor (Cash collected from vendor's debtors)			31	Preliminary Expenses			6 420·00
			41 070·00	31	Balance		c/d	42 606·75
			£139 070·00					£139 070·00
Feb. 1	Balance	b/d	42 606·75					

LEDGER
Vendor, Joseph Andrews

19 ..			£	19 ..				£
Jan. 1	Ordinary Share Capital	J	50 000·00	Jan. 1	Balance	J		135 000·00
	10% Debentures	J	35 000·00	31	Cash	CB		41 070·00
30	Cash	CB	50 000·00					
31	Cash	CB	40 043·25					
	2½% commission on debtors	J	1 026·75					
			£176 070·00					£176 070·00

Ordinary Share Capital

19 ..			£	19 ..				£
				Jan. 1	Vendor: J. Andrews	J		50 000·00
				30	Cash: Application and Allotment	CB		98 000·00
								£148 000·00

10% Debentures

19 ..			£	19 ..				£
				Jan. 1	Vendor J. Andrews	J		35 000·00

Goodwill

19 . . Jan. 1	Balance	J	£ 28 890·00	19 . .			£

Commission

19 . .			£	19 . . Jan. 31	Vendor	J	£ 1 026·75

Preliminary Expenses

19 . . Jan. 31	Cash	CB	£ 6 420·00	19 . .			£

Balance Sheet of Woodcraft, Limited
as at 31st January, 19 . .

CLAIMS	£	ASSETS	£	£
Authorised Capital		*Goodwill*		
300 000 Ordinary Shares		patents, etc.		28 890·00
of £0·50 each	150 000·00	*Fixed Assets*		
		Plant	33 110·00	
Issued Capital		Furniture, etc.	18 090·00	
296 000 Ordinary Shares				51 200·00
of £0·50 each	148 000·00	*Current Assets*		
Revenue Reserves		Stock	54 910·00	
Commission Received		Cash	42 606·75	
(Profit and Loss				97 516·75
Account)	1 026·75	*Preliminary*		
Loan Capital		*Expenses*		6 420·00
10% Debentures				
350 at £100 each	35 000·00			
	£184 026·75			£184 026·75

Chapter 42   Exercises

1

(a) Show in the Balance Sheet, on the Claims side, under '*Capital Reserve—Share Premium Account*'. This is not a profit for distribution.

(b) Show a note at foot of Balance Sheet, 'Contingent Liability on Discounted Bills £2 500'. The Bills might be dishonoured on maturity.

(c) This represents part cost debentures issue. It stands as a debit balance in the ledger. It must, therefore, appear on the assets side of the Balance Sheet. It would be gradually written off to Profit and Loss Account.

(*d*) To be deducted from debtors on the assets side of the Balance Sheet. If this is an annually fluctuating figure, the necessary adjustment each year is shown in the Profit and Loss Account and is reflected in the total Provision for Bad Debts, deducted from Debtors in the Balance Sheet.

(*e*) These are expenses incurred in the formation of a company. The total figure stands as a debit balance in the ledger and, therefore, appears on the assets side of the Balance Sheet until written off.

2

Profit and Loss Account: Final Section

19 . .			£	19 . .			£
Dividend on $6\frac{1}{4}\%$ Preference shares			3 525	Net Trading Profit	b/d	29 448	
Dividend of 17% on Ordinary shares			8 041	Balance from last year	b/f	3 329	
Reserve Fund			3 000				
Goodwill			1 600				
Balance	c/d		16 611				
			£32 777				£32 777
				Balance	b/d	16 611	

Preference Shares Dividend

19 . .			£	19 . .			£
	Cash		3 525	Profit and Loss A/c			3 525
			£3 525				£3 525

Ordinary Share Dividend

19 . .			£	19 . .			£
	Cash		7 822	Profit and Loss A/c			8 041
	Unclaimed Dividends A/c		219				
			£8 041				£8 041

Unclaimed Dividends

19 . .			£	19 . .			£
				Ordinary Share Dividend			219

Reserve Fund

19 . .			£	19 . .			£
					Profit and Loss A/c		3 000

Reserve Fund Investment

19 . .			£	19 . .			£
	Cash		3 000				

Goodwill

19 . .			£	19 . .			£
					Profit and Loss A/c		1 600

Dr.			**Cash Book**				Cr.
19 . .			£	19 . .			£
	Balance	b/d	18 628		Reserve Fund Investment		3 000
					Preference Share Dividend		3 525
					Ordinary Share Dividend		7 822
					Balance	c/d	4 281
			£18 628				£18 628
	Balance	b/d	4 281				

3

Appropriation Account

19 . . Dec. 31			£	19 . . Dec. 31			£
	General Reserve		2 000		Net Trading Profit, 31st Dec.	b/d	10 480
	Proposed Dividend: 20% on Ordinary Shares		6 000				
	Balance	c/d	2 480				
			£10 480				£10 480
				19 . . Jan. 1	Balance	b/d	2 480

Balance Sheet of A. B. Engineering Co. Ltd
as at 31st December, 19 . .

CLAIMS	£	£	ASSETS	Cost £	Depreciation £	£
Authorised Capital			*Fixed Assets*			
100 000 Ordinary			Machinery and Plant	34 000	9 700	24 300
Shares of £0·50			Furniture and Fittings	3 000	800	2 200
each		50 000				
				37 000	10 500	26 500
Issued Capital			*Current Assets*			
60 000 Ordinary			Stock, 31st December		7 400	
Shares of £0·50			Debtors		4 780	
each fully paid		30 000	Cash at Bank and in			
Revenue Reserves			hand		9 140	
General Reserve	7 000					
Profit and Loss					21 320	
Account	2 480		*Current Liabilities*			
		9 480	Creditors	2 340		
			Proposed Dividends	6 000		
					8 340	
			Working Capital			12 980
Capital Employed		£39 480	Net Value of Assets			£39 480

Alternative Method

Balance Sheet of A. B. Engineering Co. Ltd
as at 31st December, 19 . .

	Cost £	Aggregate Depreciation £	£
Fixed Assets			
Machinery and Plant	34 000	9 700	24 300
Furniture and Fittings	3 000	800	2 200
	37 000	10 500	26 500
Current Assets			
Stock	7 400		
Debtors	4 780		
Cash at Bank and in hand	9 140		
		21 320	
Current Liabilities			
Creditors	2 340		
Proposed Dividends (Gross)	6 000		
		8 340	
Working Capital			12 980
Net Assets			£39 480

	Authorised £	Issued and fully paid £
Represented by:		
Share Capital		
100 000 Ordinary Shares of £0·50 each	50 000	
60 000 Ordinary Shares of £0·50 each		30 000
Revenue Reserves		
General Reserve	7 000	
Profit and Loss Account	2 480	
		9 480
Members' Interest		£39 480

Profit and Loss Account

	£	£
Net Trading Profit		10 480
Appropriations of Profit		
General Reserve	2 000	
Proposed Dividends of 20% on Ordinary		
Shares	6 000	
		8 000
Balance carried forward		£2 480

4

Balance Sheet of Alma Manufacturing Co. Ltd
as at 31st December, 19 . .

CLAIMS	£	£	ASSETS	£	£	£
uthorised Capital			Goodwill			10 000
0 000 Ordinary Shares			*Fixed Assets*			
of £1 each	80 000		Leasehold Premises		6 700	
			Plant and Machinery		7 800	
						14 500
sued Capital						
0 000 Ordinary Shares			*Investments*			
of £1 each fully called	50 000		Investments			4 000
Less Calls in Arrear	250		*Current Assets*			
		49 750	Stock, 31st Dec.		36 297	
evenue Reserves			Debtors	16 071		
Profit and Loss Account:			*Less* Provision for			
Net Trading Profit	9 793		Bad Debts	800		
Less Interim Dividend					15 271	
paid	4 975		Cash at Bank		3 400	
		4 818	Cash in hand		100	
					55 068	
			Current Liabilities			
			Creditors		29 000	
			Working Capital			26 068
apital Employed		£54 568	Net Value of Assets			£54 568

5

Balance Sheet of A. B. Ltd
as at 31st December, 19 . .

CLAIMS	£	£	ASSETS	Cost £	Depreciation £	£
Authorised and Issued			Goodwill			10 0C
Capital			*Fixed Assets*			
20 000 Ordinary			Freehold Premises	10 000	200	9 8C
Shares of £1			Machinery	8 500	1 700	6 8C
each fully paid		20 000				
Capital Reserves				185 000	1 900	26 6C
Ordinary Share						
Premium		10 000	*Current Assets*			
Revenue Reserves			Stock, 31st Dec.		2 270	
General Reserve	1 000		Debtors	7 975		
Profit and Loss			*Less* Provision for			
Account	2 000		Bad Debts	50		
	———	3 000			7 925	
			Cash at Bank	1 405		
			Cash in hand	120		
					1 525	
					11 720	
			Current Liabilities			
			Creditors	4 820		
			Provision for Dividend	1 000		
					5 820	
			Working Capital			5 9●
			Preliminary Expenses			5●
		£33 000				£33 0●

6

Balance Sheet of C. D. Ltd
as at 30th June, 19 . .

Claims	£	£	Assets	£ Cost	£ Depreciation	£
Authorised and Issued			*Fixed Assets*			
Capital			Leasehold Premises	42 000	8 000	34 000
50 000 5% Preference			Machinery	126 056	16 056	110 000
Shares of £1			Equipment and Tools	10 763	5 382	5 381
each fully paid	50 000		Office Furniture	2 978	952	2 026
Less Calls in Arrear	150			181 797	30 390	151 407
		49 850				
100 000 Ordinary			*Current Assets*			
Shares of £1 each			Stocks, 30th June		15 826	
fully paid		100 000	Debtors		37 377	
			Cash at Bank	11 000		
		149 850	Cash in hand	255		
Revenue Reserves					11 255	
General Reserve	30 000					
Profit and Loss					64 458	
Account	23 739		*Current Liabilities*			
		53 739	Creditors		14 326	
			Working Capital			50 132
			Preliminary Expenses			2 050
Capital Employed		£203 589				£203 589

7   **Balance Sheet of Beta Gamma Ltd**
                                         as at 31st December, 19..

CLAIMS	£	£	ASSETS	Cost £	Depreciation £	£
Authorised Capital			Goodwill			9 000
40 000 6% Preference			*Fixed Assets*			
Shares of £1			Plant and Machinery	32 300	3 000	29 300
each		40 000	Fixtures and Fittings	600	30	570
236 000 Ordinary			Vans and Lorries	3 940	440	3 500
Shares of £0·25						
each		59 000		36 840	3 470	42 370
20 000 Deferred						
Shares of £0·05			*Current Assets*			
each		1 000	Stock, 31st Dec.		29 388	
		£100 000	Debtors	11 396		
			Less Provision for			
			Bad Debts	620		
					10 776	
Issued Capital			Cash at Bank		5 605	
20 000 6% Preference						
Shares of £1 each					45 769	
fully paid	20 000		*Current Liabilities*			
216 000 Ordinary			Creditors		4 597	
Shares of £0·25						
each fully paid	54 000		*Working Capital*			41 172
20 000 Deferred						
Shares of £0·05						
each	1 000					
		75 000				
Capital Reserves						
Premium on						
Preference Shares		1 000				
Revenue Reserves						
Profit and Loss						
Account	8 142					
Less Six Months'						
Dividend on the						
Preference Shares						
paid on 31st						
Oct., 19..	600					
		7 542				
Capital Employed		£83 542	Net Value of Assets			£83 542

Note to 7.

	Journal Opening Entries	Dr.	Cr.
19..		£	£
Mar. 31	Assets acquired	51 471	
	Goodwill	9 000	
	Creditors		5 471
	Vendor: Purchase price consisting of:		
	Deferred Shares		1 000
			6 471
	The *Balance* in Ordinary Shares		54 000
	(total purchase price £55 000)		
		£60 471	£60 471

Trading and Profit and Loss Account
for year ended 31st December, 19..

	£	£	£		£	£
k, 1st January			214 210·00	Sales	782 260·00	
chases		549 300·00		*Less* Returns	4 710·00	
Carriage						777 550·00
wards		3 970·00		Gross Loss c/d		12 742·50
		553 270·00				
Returns		5 210·00				
			548 060·00			
			762 270·00			
Stock, 31st Dec.			144 190·00			
			618 080·00			
ges			154 730·00			
nufacturing						
penses			9 650·00			
t, Light and						
el (Factory)			3 820·00			
reciation:						
achinery		4 612·50				
ose Tools:						
st Dec.	9 600·00					
st Jan.	9 000·00					
		600·00				
			4 012·50			
			£790 292·50			£790 292·50
ss Loss b/d			12 742·50	Discounts		2 140·00
aries			19 380·00	Account		
ectors' Fees			10 000·00	Transfer Fees		60·00
es and Insurance		9 680·00		Apprentices'		
Prepayment		1 190·00		Premiums		2 500·00
			8 490·00	Net Loss		75 047·50
ice Expenses			6 470·00			
citors' Fees			1 250·00			
airs to Buildings			6 860·00			
Debts			2 310·00			
vision for Bad						
ebts			3 240·00			
rest and Bank						
arges			980·00			
benture Interest			3 500·00			
preciation:						
otor Lorries		4 400·00				
xtures and						
ittings		125·00				
			4 525·00			
			£79 747·50			£79 747·50

Balance Sheet of the Chromium Steel Co. Ltd.
as at 31st December, 19..

CLAIMS	£	£	£
Authorised Capital			
200 000 6% Preference Shares of £1 each		200 000·00	
300 000 Ordinary Shares of £1 each		300 000·00	
		£500 000·00	
Issued Capital			
100 000 Preference Shares of £1 each fully paid		100 000·00	
175 000 Ordinary Shares of £1 each fully called	175 000·00		
Less Calls in Arrear	620·00	174 380·00	
		274 380·00	
Revenue Reserves			
Profit and Loss Account (Adverse Balance)		[75 047·50]	
		199 332·50	
Loan Capital			
500 7% Debentures of £100 each	50 000·00		
Bank Loan	24 120·00		
		74 120·00	
		£273 452·50	

ASSETS	£ Cost	£ Depreciation	£
Goodwill			50 000·00
Fixed Assets			
Freehold Factory	39 460·00		39 460·00
Plant and Machinery	61 500·00	4 612·50	56 887·50
Motor Lorries	22 000·00	4 400·00	17 600·00
Fixtures and Fittings	2 500·00	125·00	2 375·00
	£175 460·00	£9 137·50	£166 322·50
Investments			30 100·00
Current Assets			
Loose Tools, 31st December		9 600·00	
Stock, 31st December		144 190·00	
Debtors	144 800·00		
Less Provision for Bad Debts	7 240·00	137 560·00	
Rates and Insurance prepaid		1 190·00	
Cash		42 940·00	
		335 480·00	
Current Liabilities			
Creditors	203 530·00		
Bills Payable	51 420·00		
Debenture Interest due	3 500·00	258 450·00	
Working Capital			77 030·00
			£273 452·50

Alternative Method

Trading and Profit and Loss Account
for year ended 31st December, 19 . .

	£	£	£
Sales: *Less* Returns			777 550·00
Cost of Sales			
Stock, *1st January*		214 210·00	
Purchases: *Less* Returns	544 090·00		
Add Carriage Inwards	3 970·00		
		548 060·00	
		762 270·00	
Less Stock, 31st December		144 190·00	
		618 080·00	
Manufacturing Wages		154 730·00	
Manufacturing Expenses		9 650·00	
Factory Heating, Lighting, and Fuel		3 820·00	
Depreciation on Machinery		4 612·50	
		790 892·50	
Add Loose Tools, 1st January		9 000·00	
		799 892·50	
Deduct Loose Tools, 31st December		9 600·00	
			790 292·50
Gross Loss			12 742·50
Expenditure:			
Administration			
Directors' Fees		10 000·00	
Salaries		19 380·00	
Office Expenses		6 470·00	
Rates and Insurance	9 680·00		
Less Prepayment	1 190·00		
		8 490·00	
Solicitors' Fees		1 250·00	
Repairs to Buildings		6 860·00	
Finance			
Debenture Interest		3 500·00	
Interest and Bank Charges		980·00	
Bad Debts		2 310·00	
Provision for Bad Debts		3 240·00	
Provision for Depreciation:			
Motor Lorries	4 400·00		
Fixtures and Fittings	125·00		
		4 525·00	
			67 005·00
			79 747·50
Receipts			
Discounts Account		2 140·00	
Transfer Fees		60·00	
Apprentices' Premiums		2 500·00	
			4 700·00
Net Loss			£75 047·50

Alternative Method
Balance Sheet of The Chromium Steel Co. Ltd
as at 31st December, 19 . .

	Cost £	Aggregate Depreciation £	£
Goodwill	50 000·00		50 000·00
Fixed Assets			
Freehold Property	39 460·00		39 460·00
Plant and Machinery	61 500·00	4 612·50	56 887·50
Motor Lorries	22 000·00	4 400·00	17 600·00
Fixtures and Fittings	2 500·00	125·00	2 375·00
	£175 460·00	£9 137·50	£166 322·50
Investments			30 100·00
			196 422·50
Current Assets			
Loose Tools	9 600·00		
Stock	144 190·00		
Trade Debtors[1]	137 560·00		
Sundry Debtors[2]	1 190·00		
Cash at Bank	42 940·00		
		335 480·00	
Current Liabilities			
Trade Creditors	203 530·00		
Sundry Creditors[3]	3 500·00		
Bills Payable	51 420·00		
		258 450·00	
Working Capital		77 030·00	
Long-Term Liabilities			
500 7% Debentures of £100 each	50 000·00		
Bank Loan	24 120·00		
		74 120·00	
			2 910·00
Net Assets			£199 332·50

	Authorised £	Issued £
Represented by:		
Share Capital		
6% Preference Shares of £1 each	200 000·00	100 000·00
Ordinary Shares	300 000·00	175 000·00
	500 000·00	275 000·00
Calls on Ordinary Shares in Arrear		620·00
		274 380·00
Revenue Reserves		
Profit and Loss Account (Adverse Balance)		[75 047·50]
Members' Interest		£199 332·50

Notes:

		£	£
1.	Trade Debtors	144 800	
	Less Provision for Bad Debts	7 240	
			137 560
2.	Rates and Insurance Prepaid		1 190
3.	Debenture Interest due		3 500

9

Trading and Profit and Loss Account
for year ended 31st December, 19 . .

		£	£			£	£
...ock, 1st Jan.			3 000	Sales		35 000	
...rchases		28 500		*Less* Returns		650	
...ss Returns		150					34 350
			28 350				
			31 350				
...ss Stock, 31st Dec.			4 500				
...st of Sales			26 850				
...oss Profit	c/d		7 500				
			£34 350				£34 350
...nt Payable			600	Gross Profit	b/d		7 500
...tes		240		Rent Receivable		400	
...ss Amount Prepaid		40		*Add* Amount due		50	
			200				450
...laries			3 520	Discounts Account			200
...neral Expenses			250				
...vertising		300					
...ss Prepayment		100					
			200				
...d Debts written off			400				
...preciation, Fix-							
...ures and Fittings			170				
...t Trading Profit	c/d		2 810				
			£8 150				£8 150
...terim Dividend paid			750	Net Trading Profit	b/d		2 810
...ansferred to				Balance brought			
...eneral Reserve			1 000	forward 1st Jan.			5 150
...lance	c/d		6 210				
			£7 960				£7 960
				Balance	b/d		´6 210

Balance Sheet of Derry Ltd
as at 31st December, 19..

CLAIMS	£	£		ASSETS	£	Cost £	Depreciation £	£
Authorised Capital				*Goodwill*				5 000
25 000 Ordinary Shares of £1 each		25 000		*Fixed Assets*				
				Fixtures and Fittings		1 700	340	1 360
								6 360
Issued Capital								
15 000 Ordinary Shares of £1 each	15 000			*Current Assets*				
Less Uncalled amount	3 750			Stock, 31st Dec.	5 500			
		11 250		Debtors		4 500		
				Less Provision for Bad Debts	450			
Revenue Reserve						5 050		
Profit and Loss Account	6 210			*Payments in Advance*				
General Reserve	1 000			Rates	40			
		7 210		Advertising to appear next year	100			
				Rent Receivable due	50			
						190		
				Cash at Bank		4 250		
				Cash in hand		260		
							14 250	
				Current Liabilities				
				Creditors			2 150	
				Working Capital				12 100
Capital Employed		£18 460		Net Value of Assets				£18 460

Trading and Profit and Loss Account
for year ended 31st December, 19 . .

	Spares £	Petrol £	Total £		Repairs £	Petrol £	Total £
Opening Stocks, 1st Jan.	5 910	1 270	7 180	Sales	80 110	59 700	139 810
Purchases	13 260	52 680	65 940				
	19 170	53 950	73 120				
Less Stocks, 31st Dec.	4 670	2 200	6 870				
	14 500	51 750	66 250				
Wages (Repairs and Petrol Dept.)	29 480	3 160	32 640				
	43 980	54 910	98 890				
Gross Profit	36 130	4 790	40 920				
	£80 110	£59 700	£139 810		£80 110	£59 700	£139 810

	Petrol £	Total £		Petrol £	Total £
Rates		630	Gross Profit	b/d	40 920
Salaries		9 240			
Insurance	720				
Less Prepayment	120	600			
Light, Heat and Power		970			
Office Expenses		480			
General Expenses		490			
Depreciation:					
Plant and Machinery	2 500				
Petrol Pumps	1 500	4 000			
Provision for Bad Debts		200			
Net Trading Profit c/d		24 310			
		£40 920			£40 920

	Total £			Total £
Provision for 5% Dividend on the called up Capital (Tax ignored)	2 500	Net Trading Profit	b/d	24 310
Balance c/d	36 010	Balance from last year	b/f	14 200
	£38 510			£38 510
		Balance	b/d	36 010

See Chapter 10 No. 4 and Chapter 21. No. 6, for alternative method.

Balance Sheet of the Loamshire Garage Ltd
as at 31st December, 19 . .

CLAIMS	£	£	ASSETS	Cost £	Depreciation £	£
Authorised and Issued Capital			*Fixed Assets*			
50 000 Ordinary Shares of £1 each fully called	50 000		Premises	42 000		42 000
			Plant and Machinery	25 000	5 000	20 000
Less Calls in Arrear	250		Petrol Pumps	10 000	3 000	7 000
		49 750		77 000	8 000	69 000
Revenue Reserves						
Profit and Loss A/c		36 010	*Current Assets*			
			Stock		6 870	
			Debtors	5 720		
			Less Provision for Bad Debts	200		
					5 520	
			Insurance prepaid		120	
			Cash at Bank		8 500	
			Cash in hand		910	
					21 920	
			Current Liabilities			
			Provision for 5% Dividend	2 500		
			Creditors	2 660		
					5 160	
			Working Capital			16 760
		£85 760				£85 760

11

Calculations
Cash

1979			£	1979			£
Jan. 1	Balance	b/d	24 800	Jan./			
Jan./				Dec.	Creditors		579 460
Dec.	Debtors		852 400		Expenses		88 240
Dec. 31	Bank overdraft	c/d	90 500		New plant		200 000
					New premises		100 000
			£967 700				£967 700
				1980			
				Jan. 1	Bank overdraft	b/d	90 500

Control Account

1979			£	1979			£
Jan. 1	Balance	b/d	32 480	Dec. 31	Balance	c/d	62 480
Dec. 31	Sales		882 400	31	Cash		852 400
			£914 880				£914 880

Creditors Control Account

1979			£	1979			£
Dec. 31	Balance	c/d	102 560	Jan. 1	Balance	b/d	52 700
31	Cash		579 460	Dec. 31	Current Liabilities		629 320
			£682 020				£682 020

Trading and Profit and Loss Account
for year ended 31st December, 1979

	£			£
Stock 1st January 1979	48 120	Sales		882 400
Wages and materials	629 320			
Depreciation	63 300			
	740 740			
Less Stock 31st December	82 200			
	658 540			
Gross Profit c/d	223 860			
	882 400			882 400
Expenses	88 240	Gross Profit	b/d	223 860
Net Profit	219 820	Balance 31.12.78	b/d	84 200
	£308 060			£308 060

Balance Sheet
as at 31st December, 1979

	£	£		£	£
Share Capital			*Fixed Assets*		
360,000 Ordinary share			Freehold Premises	200 000	
of £1 each		360 000	*Add* New premises	100 000	
Profit and Loss Account		219 820			300 000
			Plant	306 400	
Current Liabilities			*Add* new plant	200 000	
Creditors	102 560				506 400
Bank overdraft	90 500		*Less* Depreciation:		
		193 060	Old plant	153 200	
			New plant	25 000	
				178 200	
					328 200
			Current Assets		
			Stock 31st December	82 200	
			Debtors	62 480	
					144 680
		£772 880			£772 880

Cash

			£					£
1980 Jan./ Dec.	Debtors		852 400	1980 Dec. 31 Jan./ Dec.	Bank overdraft	b/d		90 500
					Creditors			579 460
					Expenses			88 240
					Balance	c/d		94 200
1981			£852 400					£852 400
Jan. 1	Balance	b/d	94 200					

Chapter 43   Exercises

1. See pages 462, 463 of textbook.

2. See page 462.

3. See page 463.

4. See page 465.

5. (*a*), (*b*), (*c*) see pages 464–465.

6. See page 464.

7. See page 462.